FROM THE KRAAL
TO THE CATHEDRAL

❖ ❖ ❖

FROM THE KRAAL TO THE CATHEDRAL

❖ ❖ ❖

The Memoir of Daniel Deng Bul Yak,
Archbishop of Sudan

DANIEL DENG BUL YAK

Foreword by Justin Welby, Archbishop of Canterbury

ISBN 978-0-69207-849-5

Table of Contents

A gallery of images follows page 44

Foreword

When I was appointed to my role as Archbishop of Canterbury, I felt prompted to visit and acquaint myself with all the thirty-seven other primates (lead bishops) of the provinces of the Anglican Communion in their own provinces within the first eighteen months of my archiepiscopacy. The Province of South Sudan and Sudan was very high up in my mind, given the history of violence there: long wars leading to the independence of South Sudan, followed by internal fighting *between* factions of the newly independent South Sudan.

In January 2014 Caroline, my wife, and I embarked on a three-day visit to Archbishop Daniel and Mama Deborah, the bishops and their wives, and the Church of the Province. Two days before we got to the South Sudan, Archbishop Daniel rang and asked that we visit Bor, about 149 kilometers north of Juba, and with some of his bishops. One of my tweets from Bor, on 31 January 2014, summarizes the impression the visit left on us: "Bor—shattered vehicles, bodies in streets, looted, a place of evil deeds. Asked to bless mass grave before use."

Another indelible impression was hearing Archbishop Daniel plead with the survivors to forgive. What we saw in Bor that day was truly devastating. The truth must be established, the victims recognized, and the suffering acknowledged. Establishing the truth has to be the first step towards reconciliation. We are called to tell the truth in love. We need to grow closer to Jesus Christ. Only Jesus Christ can change the situation and change human hearts. His own prayer was "Father forgive." The promise of the Holy Spirit warms in us the love of those who do us harm.

I have watched Archbishop Deng, a Dinka, one of the major ethnic groups involved in the conflict, bravely assume the sensitive and delicate role of a mediating pastor in the South Sudan conflict. He has sometimes been accused of being partisan by people from other ethnic groups, and accused of inadequate sympathy by people of his own ethnic group!

Mediating for reconciliation is about being a bridge—and being a bridge means that you get walked on. Yet his position remains that "someone has to play that role." The role is complex, heavy, and uncertain. There is criticism and doubt, yet he is a man who takes the Christian mandate for reconciliation seriously and has held fast to his calling.

The Province of South Sudan is one I care much about. It heartens me to see unity in the House of Bishops and a measure of collaboration among the churches and with aid agencies. That unity is more and more strained by the intolerable pressures of war. It continues to be my prayer that the Church united would continue to engage with civil authority and the people of South Sudan, and increase its prophetic role in the conflict. Truth should increasingly, pre-emptively be told to the leaders and the led.

I use the platform of this book to once more appeal to the leaders of the nation to be mindful of their ignoble roles in perpetuating this conflict. They must all be mindful of the fact that we shall all give account to our Maker for what we have done here on earth. We serve God who gave His Son Jesus Christ for our sins; our response must be both repentance and imitation of His sacrifice.

Given the circumstances the Provinces of South Sudan and Sudan find themselves in, I must commend Archbishop Daniel Deng Bul Yak, his brother the Archbishop of the new Province of Sudan, Archbishop Ezekiel Kondo, and the rest of the bishops, for keeping the church going in various states of existence. With some bishops forced to live outside their sees and only able to make occasional visits, congregations separated by the instability of sporadic fighting, vast populations unable to plant and reap, and millions of refugees, the province has been sustained by God's grace and the determination of his people living out the Gospel, wherever they are.

The Right Honourable and Most Reverend Justin Welby
Archbishop of Canterbury
Lambeth Palace, London
September 15, 2017

Preface

I have heard it said that secretly, each of us believes that he or she is the most important character in the story of life. And certainly, the way we experience our lives may lead us to sincerely think that we are at the center of everything. However, as my life has unfolded, it is plain to me that actually, the most important character in my story is Almighty God, the creator of the heavens and the earth, as He has revealed Himself in the person and work of Jesus Christ.

St. Paul, in his letter to the church at Ephesus, says that we are "God's handiwork, created in Christ Jesus to do good works, which God prepared in advance for us to do" (Ephesians 2:10, NIV). This truth reminds me that I am actually only one of many characters in the unfolding drama of God's creation. It also reminds me that my place in the drama has been established by God, the great Author of the story of creation. And as I look back on my life, I can only confess that Almighty God has indeed provided for me, protected me, empowered me, encouraged me, and preserved my life, even to this day. There is, quite simply, no other explanation for even my survival, much less for anything I have been able to accomplish along the way.

How else can I explain how, though being born at one of the most violent moments in one of the most violent nations on earth, my heart should still seek restlessly for peace and for a way to foster peace between warring peoples? How else can I account for the way that so many opportunities and blessings have been placed before me, despite living in a land that has seemed bent on tearing itself apart for more than six decades? As I review the course of my life, I can only marvel at the many ways that God has intervened, at just the right time and in just the right way, to permit me to live to see another day in which I might seek to do his will.

By the grace of God, I have come from the poorest of circumstances to a position where I can serve and work for the improvement of the lives of people who still live in danger, fear, and vulnerability. I have been preserved through war, famine, and persecution so that I might become an advocate for peace, plenty, and tolerance. I have faced great danger and harsh oppression, and these severe masters have taught me patience, persistence, and reliance on the Almighty. I was born without the protection of a father, but the Father above has permitted me to become a spiritual father and protector to thousands of people who are unable to protect themselves. Truly, I have much to be thankful for, for which I offer praise to God, through our Lord Jesus Christ.

Sudan, the largest country in Africa before its division in 2011, is a place of immensity and contrast. In the north lie vast deserts, part of the southeastern reaches of the Sahara. In the south, dense forests and nearly impenetrable swamplands cover the landscape. In the north, much of the population is Muslim, consisting of Arabic speakers whose forebears, in the majority, migrated south into the region from Egypt and Arabia, along the Nile valleys, starting as early as the eighth century after Christ, by some accounts. In the south, the people, most descended from Nilotic tribes who migrated eastward into the Nile region perhaps as early as the first century, are predominantly Christian or follow traditional African animistic religions.

Because of such wide differences between large segments of its people, the history of my homeland has all too often been dominated by misunderstanding, repression, and even bloodshed. And yet, one of the most important guiding principles of my life has been framed by the words of Jesus, "Blessed are the peacemakers." If everyone merely accepts that violence and bloodshed are inevitable, then, without question, they become inevitable. But I cannot accept this. I believe that peace and understanding between people is possible, whether they are separated by religious beliefs, tribal rivalries, political differences, or even the common, day-to-day misunderstandings that occur in every society, family, and workplace. Mind you, peace is frequently not easy to achieve, because first, people must put aside their long-learned mistrust and their preconceptions about those on the other side. And yet, time and again in my life and ministry, I have seen that with the proper encouragement, people who were enemies can become, if not friends, then at least co-participants in building a future based on peace and tolerance, rather than violence and repression.

I hope that by telling the story of my life journey, I can encourage others to become workers for peace and reconciliation. I do not wish to hold myself up as anything other than a simple man who has tried, in every circumstance, to find a way forward—a way toward peace, security, human dignity, and furtherance of the way of life to which all of us are called by God. These goals have guided my journey, and if by telling my story I can encourage others to share these principles, that will be the best outcome I could hope for.

As I begin this work, I want to acknowledge Reverend John Dau, an esteemed brother in the faith who first encouraged me to write down my story. I also thank Gachora Ngunjiri, a dear friend who began encouraging me, years ago, to write down my story with the aim of sharing it with others who might find it useful in some way. I am deeply grateful to Miss Jane Amito, who carefully typed the earliest drafts of this book, and also to Mr. Richard Rugya, who was very helpful in assisting me with thinking through how the book should be organized.

I am grateful for the efforts of Jane Sell and Philip Berke, my dear friends in Texas, who kindly agreed to inquire among their friends and acquaintances for a writer who could help me develop my memoirs into book form. They introduced me to Thom Lemmons, who has worked very hard to organize my thoughts and stories into the words you are reading now, and I am very thankful for his many efforts.

Jane and Philip's son, Timothy Berke, was the college roommate of my son, Peter. During their time in college, they became more like brothers than friends, so much so that Timothy came back to South

Sudan after his graduation in order to help me in my work for peace and reconciliation. Needless to say, there were many more inviting places in the world that Tim could have gone to begin his career, but I will always be thankful that he came here to aid those of us who are trying to rebuild our troubled country.

As in every undertaking of my life, I owe a debt of thanks to my dear wife, Mrs. Deborah Abuk Atem Mading, who has been my steadfast partner through all the difficulties and the blessings of the years. And I am also thankful for my children—Grace, Martha, Peter, Emmanuel, Awaak, and Isaac—for the joy they have brought into my life and the source of pride they continue to be. I am especially proud of Peter, who returned from the United States, after completing his studies there, to take up the difficult work of aiding in the renewal of South Sudan.

Finally, I dedicate this book to the memory of my blessed mother, Mrs. Myabol Ajang Diing, who gave me life and who also taught me my earliest lessons in how to live. Without her, I would never have been able to do anything that I have done. And I also dedicate this work, as I have dedicated my entire life, to Almighty God, in whom and for whom I have my very being.

FROM THE KRAAL
TO THE CATHEDRAL

❖ ❖ ❖

CHAPTER 1

Born into a Nation at War

I was born in 1950, five years before the world began to end—at least, the world that I knew. At the time of my birth, the British-Egyptian condominium agreement by which Sudan had been administered since 1898 was in the process of being dismantled.[1] This transition from colonial government to self-rule was especially difficult for my country because of the wide differences in culture and concentration of power between the northern and southern regions. As happens all too often in such contexts, the vacuum left by the withdrawal of colonialist administration and military forces created a situation that was ripe for exploitation by regional factions with little interest in governance that did not advance their personal and immediate aims.

❖ ❖ ❖

I entered the world in Pawooi, a small village of the Awulial clan, located in what is now the Republic of South Sudan. Powoi is in an area called Twic East County—though at that time it was called Kongor District—which in turn is in Jonglei State, slightly east of the center of South Sudan. My tribe, the Jieng, is one of many groups belonging to the sub-Saharan Nilotic culture whose forebears migrated from somewhere in western Africa into the Nile basin, perhaps before the first century A.D.[2] The traditional Nilotic culture is pastoralist, depending heavily for subsistence upon cattle grazing and cultivation of cereal crops such as sorghum, millet, and rice. Such a way of living lends itself to the loosely organized, semi-nomadic patterns that characterize the Nilotic peoples of South Sudan.

It is impossible for me to overstate the importance of cattle in traditional Nilotic culture. Among the Jieng (or Dinka, as others often call us), we have a saying: "If the cattle die, the people die." Boys and young men, who are entrusted with the care of the cattle upon the grazing grounds, memorize the lineage and bloodlines of each animal in their custody. In South Sudan, each cow and bull has both a given name and a family name, just as humans do; it is not at all uncommon for a boy—who may not be able to read or write—to be able to recite, not only the names of the cattle for which he is responsible, but also the names of each animal's sire and dam, and their sires and dams in turn, as much as five or six generations back. To this day, the principal indicator of wealth in South Sudan—especially in Jieng communities—even among the educated and professional classes in the cities, is cattle ownership.

It is perhaps not surprising, given the preeminence of cattle in South Sudanese culture, that cattle raiding between clans also has a long history. Typically, such conflicts were small in scale and localized, occurring most often during the dry season, when people living in more arid regions moved their herds toward areas with more water and better grazing. This movement often resulted in skirmishes with those already settled in well-watered areas. Traditionally, cattle raiding was seen as a rite of passage for boys who sought to become recognized as men. Tragically, in recent years, with the legacy of decades of civil war, chronic food and water shortages, and intertribal hostility, cattle raiding has become more frequent, large-scale, and violent.[3]

As if this were not bad enough, during the years of intense civil and military strife between northern and southern Sudan, agents provocateurs working for various northern interests were often able to take advantage of tribal hostilities to divide and destabilize southern Sudanese society. All too often, with the encouragement or incitement provided by these northern sympathizers, groups in the south would turn on each other, doing as much or more damage to themselves as anything inflicted by the north. This pattern became well established early in the history of Sudan, and it has repeated itself all too often throughout the many years of struggle.

The family I was born into was situated in the midst of traditional Jieng culture. As an infant and a young boy, I inherited the animistic religious beliefs of the Nilotic peoples. In fact, the story of my birth is indelibly stamped with my Jieng origins. Had I been born under the same circumstances but in a different place and time, I would have been the son of a different father.

The man I came to know as my father, Bul de Yak, died long before I was born—before I was even conceived. In traditional Jieng culture, however, the brother of a deceased Jieng man has a responsibility to care for his brother's widow, and this responsibility includes providing progeny. And so it was that my uncle, Biar de Yak de Biar, and my mother, Myabol Ajang Diing, gave life to me, and I became the last-born son of Bul de Yak. Actually, my mother gave birth to twins, but my brother, who was named Mabil, died barely a week after we were born.

As the youngest child, I depended for my upbringing not only upon my mother, but also upon my older siblings. My father had two wives: my mother and Ngaar Malual, my stepmother, whose children were also my brothers and sisters. All that I know of my father I learned from the other people in my family. Sadly, none of the children of my stepmother are still alive; her last surviving child died in 2004. Of the children of my mother, only my older brother Malual Thii and I are still living.

My father, Bul de Yak, was a magician, or what might be called a shaman—"Malual," as such people are called in the Jieng tongue. By all accounts, he was highly regarded in our village as a problem-solver and an honest, peace-loving person. People came to him with all sorts of difficulties, and he would do what he could to help them. Women who were barren, for example, would come to my father for prayers and rituals that, they believed, would help them conceive children. Any child subsequently resulting from such intercession by my father would be named "Malual" or "Alual," names indicating that the magician had successfully aided in bringing the child into being.

My mother and my brothers, Malual and Agok, who were still at home at the time, told me much about my father. They assured me that he was a refined gentleman who was respected by the people in Pawooi. Nevertheless, our lives were difficult during my early days, because of our lack of cattle. It seems that prior to my father's death, he gave two cows to my mother's brother, but when my father died, the cows were not returned. My brother petitioned our uncle for the return of the cows, since they were our only means of upkeep, but these efforts were unsuccessful. Ultimately, my brother, at the tender age of 15, had to go with my mother to court in order to obtain the return of my father's cattle. After due deliberation, the court ordered that the cows be returned to us, and we had a new lease on life. Perhaps as a result of such difficulties, however, my brother Agok had left Pawooi previously, traveling to a larger city to seek a better life.

❖❖❖

In contrast to the south, northern Sudan is mostly arid, desert country, populated by Arabic-speaking persons. Beginning in perhaps the eighth century A.D., groups from Egypt and Arabia began moving down the Nile into what later became Sudan, bringing with them Arabic and Islamic culture and beliefs. Indeed, the non-African, Arabic influence is apparent, even in the name of the nation: "Bilad al-Sudan," the name Arab immigrants gave to the territory they were entering, means "land of the black people."

Muslim expansion into northern Africa began soon after the Arabian peninsula was united under the teachings and political leadership of Mohammed, in the middle of the seventh century A.D. By the eighth century, North African Muslims began exploring the Nile Valley and creating trade routes, spurred by their interest in ivory and slaves. They took both from the southern region of Sudan.

Coming from a culture with an organized central government,

generally more advanced technology, and a military tradition of conquest, the immigrants from the north typically treated the black African peoples of the south with contempt, seeing them as pagan savages. The more organized and stronger northwestern African kingdoms of Nubia and Makuria, Christian since the sixth century, were both eventually overwhelmed by Islam, with Makuria falling in the fourteenth century. For their part, the southern peoples, with their agrarian, semi-nomadic culture, were generally no match for the traders and raiders of the north. When they could, the Jieng, Nuer, Murle, Shilluk, and other southern tribes retreated into their swamps to evade the depredations of the invaders. When they could not, they were subdued and shackled, then sold in the slave markets.

As a result, political and military power became consolidated in the northern part of the country, with its administrative center in the city of Khartoum, located at the confluence of the Blue and White Nile Rivers. When European traders arrived in the mid-1800s, close on the heels of the Turco-Egyptian Ottoman invasion of the 1820s, they found an organized system in place by which they could exploit the resources of the south, with the Muslim rulers of the north as their partners. At the peak of the slave trade, as many as 30,000 captives were taken from the non-Muslim regions of southern Sudan each year.[4]

By the way, the name by which my tribe is most widely known has its origins in the coming of the Ottoman Empire and its control, through Egypt, over Sudan. During World War I, as Turkish soldiers were enlisting men from the south of the country to fight against the Allied powers, they asked each applicant for his family name. My last name, Deng, is very common among the Jieng people, and after many men had said "Deng" when asked for their last names, the Turks decided that all these people were from the Deng tribe—which they pronounced as "Dinka." And so, to much of the world, my people are known and referred to as "Dinka," though we refer to ourselves and our language as Jieng.

The coming of the British in 1898, and the establishment of the

Anglo-Egyptian Condominium Government—with a governor-general appointed by Egypt and approved by the British—somewhat relieved the most obvious repression of the south. Indeed, the British, partly in order to frustrate Egyptian attempts to establish political control of the entire Nile Valley, forced the administration of Sudan as two separate regions: the Arabic-speaking, Islamic north, and the animistic and increasingly Christian south, where the use of English was encouraged.

Resentment of the British seethed within the Islamic elites of Khartoum—and Cairo—based on a history of what they viewed as British intrusions, such as the installation of supposed puppet governments in Khartoum and heavy-handed imposition of Western values and governance. The British withdrew from Egypt in 1936 but still maintained a presence in Sudan, despite the outcries of successive Egyptian governments. With the revolution in 1953 that abolished the Egyptian monarchy, Gamel Abdel Nasser and other leaders in Egypt forged an agreement with London to grant independence to Sudan, both from the United Kingdom and from Egypt. They saw this as the only way to get the British to leave. Of course, Cairo had no intention of governing Sudan, given its impoverished condition when compared to Egypt. Thus, the stage was set for a power vacuum, as the British withdrew in 1955, and Egypt left Sudan to its own devices.

In southern Sudan, we viewed the leaving of the British with deep apprehension. Given the past several centuries of our history, we had every reason to fear that, absent the protection afforded by British administration and military organization, the Arab slavers would return to plunder our people and our resources.[5] Indeed, as the British departed and new officials were appointed to take their places throughout the country, the vast majority of posts were filled by Muslims, even in the predominantly non-Muslim south of the country. It seemed to many in the south that we had exchanged British and Egyptian colonialism for a new form of colonialism instigated by the Islamic north of the country. This would not be an improvement in our lot.

❖ ❖ ❖

Of course, when all this began to happen, I was only five years old. I suppose, at the time, that I knew something was brewing that disturbed my elders; children often sense such things, even when they do not have the words to understand them in the way that adults do. However, in those days I was primarily concerned with the same things that preoccupy children everywhere: playing with my friends, getting my share of food at meal times, and keeping out of trouble with my mother and my older siblings.

As I have mentioned, traditional Jieng society revolves around cattle: feeding them, tending them, milking them, and obtaining more of them, either by breeding or trade. This was certainly true for me, living in a rural village. Families with many cattle are wealthy; those with few or no cattle are poor and not respected. In the wealthy families, children are treasured and looked after. A neglected child in such a family would be considered a disgrace to the family and even to the clan. Also, in a rural village, everyone knows everyone else; all the inhabitants are typically members of the same clan. It is a very communal life, indeed.

The traditional houses of the Nilotic tribes are round, mud-brick structures with conical thatched roofs, sometimes called *tukuls*. Often, homesteads are surrounded by vegetable gardens, typically tended by the women, and are sometimes separated from each other by an open stretch of grassland or scrub forest. In villages, the houses are often closer together. Men and boys would tend the cattle, and the women and girls would work in the fields, growing millet or sorghum.

In a bush village, the nights are very dark, indeed—there are no street lights or even lamps inside the homes, for the most part. When darkness comes at about 8:00 p.m., everyone goes to bed! If the cattle are not in the cattle camp, or *kraal*, they are penned in a structure called a *luak*, built of much the same materials as a house, but usually larger. Other domesticated animals common to rural life in South Sudan, such as chickens, guineas, and goats, may also be put inside the *luak* for the night.

When I woke in the morning in my mother's *tukul*, I might eat a piece of *kuin,* a type of flatbread made from sorghum meal. In season, there might be some tomatoes, peanut paste, or rice to go along with it. I might wash my breakfast down with a few swallows of warm milk. Indeed, one of the reasons cattle are so important in the pastoral culture of sub-Saharan Africa is because they provide so much of what is necessary to sustain life. Milk, meat, hides, and even their dung—which, when dried, can be burned as fuel to provide warmth and also protection from insects—are staples of daily life in a rural village.

Those without cattle are forced to rely on what may be gathered from the forest. Desert dates (*thaau* in Jieng), leaves of the cadaba bush (*anaat*) or spiderflower (*acuiol*), berries of the Christ's-thorn (*lang*), cross berries (*apoor*), and other plants could be used for food, but gathering them is difficult and time-consuming, and they would only be eaten when nothing else was available, as in times of famine, or if the family were poor and had no way to obtain better food.[6]

Often, young children are tasked with cleaning out the *luak* after the animals are led out. They sweep out the dung and prepare the structure to receive the animals when evening comes again.

Once my chores were completed, I might wander toward the center of the village. I would probably find boys grappling on the ground; wrestling is a very important sport in traditional Nilotic culture. I might join in for a tumble or two. Village children—especially boys—also played a game called *adau* in which a rounded piece of wood is hit with a stick. *Adau* has some similarities with soccer; it is played by two teams of about twelve players each. Because of the wooden ball, this game can be dangerous, especially when the fast-moving ball strikes a player's shin or, worse, his head.

Kuoi is a much safer game. It is played with a ring made of woven grass that is rolled back and forth between two teams of about six each. The object is to get the ring past the other team. Players use *acalual*, a type of long, sharpened stick, to nab the ring or knock it off course before it can roll past their team's goal line.

Anyau is a circle game that is something like jumping rope. An older child or possibly an adult stands in the middle of the circle, holding a long string or rope attached to a dry husk or gourd. This person then begins to twirl the husk around the circle so that centrifugal force causes the rope to become straight. The players in the circle try to jump the rope without letting it touch them. As the twirler gradually raises the height of the spinning rope, jumping it becomes more and more difficult. The winner is the one who can jump the highest.

If I didn't become involved in one of these games, I might walk over to a nearby group of older boys who were admiring the fresh scars on the forehead of their friend. He would have just received the marks of manhood from the village elders, and his friends might compliment him on his show of bravery; he likely made no sound and did not so much as wince as the elders sliced the skin of his forehead with a heated blade. Indeed, to have shown his pain would have caused him great loss of standing among the men of the village. At the ceremony marking his scarring, his father might have sacrificed a fine, red heifer to insure the favor of Nhialic, the Creator. As I listened to the telling, I might have said a silent prayer to Nhialic, asking him to make me brave when the time for my own scarring came.

In fact, life in a rural village in South Sudan can often require bravery of its children, simply in the course of everyday life. I remember one occasion, when I was about nine or ten years old, when my brother Malual told me to take a sick calf, accompanied by its mother, back to our village from the kraal. At that time, the camp was at a place called Cikaar-Anook, about twenty miles east of Pawooi. The older boys were moving the cattle almost thirty miles in the opposite direction, and Malual didn't think the calf would be able to make the journey. The calf had been injured because it had strayed onto the property of a farmer who hit it with a hoe as he was driving it away.

I began walking back from the kraal toward Pawooi, herding the calf and its mother; it was a thirteen-hour walk through the bush. By the time

I was approaching Pawooi, dark was falling. When I was still about two miles from home, I saw the shapes of five hyenas, circling around us, drawn by the scent and appearance of the injured calf.

They came closer, trying to separate the calf from its mother. The cow charged them with her horns down. In the meantime, I had found a short, stout stick and was using it to keep the hyenas at bay. The hyenas were wily; three of them came at us from the front, while two others circled around behind, trying to bring down the calf. I kept jumping back and forth, now swinging my stick at a hyena in front, then spinning around to fend off one coming from the rear. At the same time, I was yelling at the top of my lungs and beating my stick on the ground, trying to get the attention of somebody from my village.

Finally, I heard a man's voice in the distance, coming from behind me: "Stand firm! I am coming!" It was the most welcome sound I had ever heard! I kept yelling, swinging my stick at the hyenas, and throwing clods of dirt at them. When the man finally reached us, the hyenas slinked away into the dark.

Because much of South Sudan is low-lying, containing extensive marshes and swamps, it is very vulnerable to the floods that often occur during the rainy season, which lasts from May until October. In 1961, when I was eleven years old, a devastating flood occurred in my home county, Twic East. Throngs of people and cattle had to leave their homes and seek higher ground. Many went east toward the border with Ethiopia, as much as sixty-five miles, on foot and driving livestock. Some were forced into territory belonging to the Nuer, a tribe related to the Jieng, and many went south, toward Borland and Equatoria State. Many died, both humans and cattle, and the rampaging waters destroyed countless homes.

Malual and I journeyed north, taking our few cattle with us, toward the territory between Duk Padiet and the city of Malakal, on the eastern side of the White Nile, which is populated by people from the Nuer, Jieng, and Shilluk tribes. We had no particular destination in mind; we were only trying to find a place above the flood waters where our cattle could feed and we could be safe.

We came to a highway running from Malakal, in southern Upper Nile State, south to Bor, in the southwest corner of Jonglei State. This was fortunate for us, because the government had constructed the road on the highest ground available. We were even more pleased when one of the drivers of the vehicles on the highway proved to be our brother, Agok Bul Yak. He took me with him to Malakal. He left Malual to continue looking after the cattle, since he was older than I.

Not long after this, Agok was able to take me to Adong, which at that time was in the Baliet district. Adong, south and slightly east of Malakal, is in a region mostly populated by the Jieng De Padang clan of Ngok Lual Yak, a subgroup of the Jieng people. There was a boarding school there where I was able to study from about 1961 to 1964, when war intervened— as it would many times during my youth.

❖ ❖ ❖

In the late 1950s, as the British were leaving Sudan and the Islamic leaders in the north were taking control of the newly formed national government, many of the leaders of southern Sudan—educated persons who were acutely aware of the direction events were taking—fled to Uganda or went into hiding in the bush, fearing arrest or worse at the hands of the Muslim-dominated government. Before long, many of their fears began to be confirmed, as Major General Ibrahim Abbud, who had led a coup against the first democratically elected government in Khartoum, began to impose Arabic and Islamic culture on the south, believing that this was the only way to unify the nation. Arabic replaced English as the official language, and the Missionary Societies Act of 1962 severely limited the activities of Christian missionaries in the south. The Christian holy day of Sunday was changed to the Islamic holy day of Friday. It became clear to southerners that the intention of Khartoum was to make the entire country a Muslim nation—by force, if necessary.

On August 18, 1955, when I was five years old, members of the Southern Sudan Defence Forces, at that time under British administration, staged a violent mutiny in Torit, a town far to the south, in Eastern Equatoria State. Various reasons have been given for the mutiny: some have suggested that it was sparked by the arrest of a southern Sudanese member of the national assembly; others have laid the blame on a supposed telegram from Khartoum that urged the official suppression of southerners; while still others have suggested that the soldiers were being ordered north, and they became convinced that they would be going to their deaths if they obeyed. For whatever reason or combination of reasons, the soldiers seized weapons and went on a rampage in which many northerners were indiscriminately killed. With British help, the mutiny was put down, but not before many of the soldiers, including a number of officers, had fled into the bush.[7]

Thus began a period of guerilla actions of scattered bands of soldiers formerly in the Sudanese army, now fighting against the Khartoum government. The core of former military men gradually began to attract others. Especially with the increased repression from Khartoum, many students, intellectuals, former government officials, and political leaders—many of the south's current and future leaders—found the fledgling resistance movement more attractive than trying to remain in the official government and effect change from within.

Unfortunately, though the new rebels were uniformly opposed to the repression of the northern government, they soon developed rivalries among themselves. Some of these rivalries were based on tribal and ethnic mistrust, and others were simply driven by political jealousy and lust for power—what little power there was, in those very early days.

Ultimately the most successful of the anti-Khartoum organizations, the Southern Sudan Liberation Movement was organized principally by Joseph Lagu, who was a lieutenant in the Sudanese army and a member of the Madi tribe from the territory south of Juba. This group had been agitating and advocating for world attention to the plight of southern

Sudan. In 1963, a military wing of this movement called Anya Nya ("snake venom" or "scorpion venom" in the Madi tongue) achieved sufficient organization and strength to actually pose a threat. Significantly, one of Joseph Lagu's lieutenants was a young man named John Garang, who would become very important to southern Sudanese independence in years to come.

Anya Nya began to harass and attack northern army elements and police posts. By 1964, when I was in school and hoping to be able to complete my education, the First Sudanese Civil War had begun in earnest.

❖ ❖ ❖

As the violence began to intensify in and around Adong, our school was closed. This pattern would become all too familiar during the nine long years of the First Sudanese Civil War. The students were told to leave and return to their homes, using any means at their disposal. I would have to walk back to Malakal—a distance of some thirty-seven miles. Three of us—Ajang Dau Ajang, Biar Atem Ajang, and myself—set out from Adong toward Malakal. Biar was the youngest of us (today, he is a lieutenant major general in the army of South Sudan).

We came to a place called Anakdiar, about halfway between Adong and Malakal. Anakdiar is located on the Sobat River, a tributary of the White Nile. Night was coming, we were tired, and we found a place in Anakdiar to sleep.

Sometime around 3:00 a.m., we were awakened by the sound of gunfire and shouting. Startled, we leaped from our mats and looked outside to see government troops pouring from a steamer, moored at the river dock. They were firing their weapons and setting fire to the thatched roofs of the houses.

With the family that had hosted us for the night, we ran into the bush to hide from the northern soldiers. We watched, terrified, as they kept shooting and burning until almost sunup.

When the soldiers finally left, boarding the steamer and continuing south on the river toward the town of Nasir, the people of Anakdiar came out of hiding and looked helplessly at their ruined village. Human bodies and the carcasses of livestock littered the ground. Most of the houses were smoking ruins.

For the three of us, there was nothing left to do but keep walking toward Malakal—even though that was likely where the soldiers on the steamer had come from. We walked through the bush for several hours until we came to a village called Mahmmad Ajak, and then we walked for another fifteen miles or so until we reached the outskirts of Malakal. By this time, it was nearing 7:00 p.m.; we had been walking all day with no food and little water, and we were very tired.

My uncle Thuc Ajang Dau lived in Malakal. He was responsible for the upkeep of the road from Malakal to Bor. In fact, he was likely the reason my older brother Agok had left our village to seek his fortune in Malakal. My uncle had, by this time, heard of the problems around Adong and the attack on Anakdiar, and all my relatives in Malakal were very worried about our whereabouts and our safety. He was very glad to see the three bedraggled, hungry schoolboys on his doorstep, and he brought us into his home and gave us something to eat and drink.

When we had been there about a month, my brother Malual, who had originally left Pawooi with me as we tried to escape the flooding, arrived in Malakal. He told me that I was to return to our village with him—a distance of some 200 miles. It would be a long walk during the dry season, between December of 1964 and January of 1965; the journey would take fourteen days.

We set out toward the south, driving cattle along with us. Along the way, my brother and I became separated. As we passed through Nuer territory, my brother's group, which was herding the cattle, was attacked at a place called Ayuai. The cattle were stolen, and my brother sustained a serious head injury. I knew nothing of this until three days later, when we finally arrived in Pawooi.

When we had been back in our village for about three years, my older brother Malual took a wife, Nguak Akeny Lual, whose family lived in the village of Maar Payam. In order to pay the bride price customary among our people, he needed all of the cattle remaining to us; nothing was left for me, the youngest in the family. By this time, I was seventeen years old.

My options were severely limited by these circumstances. All the other young men my age were at the kraals, tending their families' herds. There was no herd for me to tend—not even a single cow. Because of this, I could not go to the cattle camp, as would have been expected for me to do.

My deepest desire was to go back to school. I had been in the third year of my studies in the Arabic school in Adong when the war caused the school's closing. I told Malual of my ambition and suggested that I travel to Bor, the capital of Jonglei State, situated in its southwestern corner, near the White Nile. In Bor, I believed I could find a school and continue my education. Also, I told him, our mother was now in Bor; I could stay with her as I went to school.

But Malual rejected my idea. His principal reason was the tremendous insecurity in the region, caused by the ongoing Anya Nya rebellion and the vicious attempts at suppression exerted by the Khartoum government. Nevertheless, I was determined to get back into school, and I knew that our mother would support my decision. I said none of this to Malual, however.

Instead, one morning very early, I left Pawooi and began walking south toward Bor, about seventy-five miles away. On the afternoon of my second day of walking, around 3:00 p.m., I met an old woman coming from the town. She warned me that Arab soldiers were there, rounding up boys my age and killing them.

Still, I had to get to Bor; my mother was there, as was my only chance at furthering my education. I continued on, despite the old woman's warning—although I went very cautiously. I reached the outskirts around 6:00 p.m. The woman who had earlier warned me against going to Bor had returned with me, out of pure compassion, I think. To my great relief, she knew where my mother lived and agreed to take me to her.

By 8:00 p.m., I was reunited with my mother. She was both overjoyed to see me and also very angry at me for coming into such danger. She blamed Malual for allowing me to make the journey. I did my best to assure her that Malual was not responsible—that, in fact, he had forbidden me to come. I also explained to her that I saw no future for myself in Pawooi, with no cattle and no prospects of acquiring any. Even in such desperate circumstances, I reasoned, people must do everything in their power to move toward hope. For me, hope lay in Bor, and especially in gaining more education. Certainly, I had placed myself at great risk, but to me at that time, it seemed a risk worth taking.

My mother hid me in a small hut and ordered me not to show my face. It became apparent that the situation in Bor was not getting any better, and my mother, with the advice of other women friends, determined that they had to get me out of Bor and back to Malakal, where my relatives were. A steamer regularly made the passage up the White Nile from Juba, south of Bor, to Malakal, far to the north. My mother thought it might be possible to smuggle me onto the steamer, disguised as a girl.

They found girl's clothes that would cover my lanky frame and a head-dress to complete the disguise. On the night of the next steamer's departure, I walked with the others who intended to board the steamer, my heart beating so loud in my chest that I thought everyone around me could surely hear it.

It was quite dark as we approached the river and the place where the steamer was docked, and yet I dared not look to the right nor the left. There were many troops guarding the steamer, and a checkpoint had been set up in front of the gangway so that everyone who boarded could be thoroughly inspected. I thought that I would surely be discovered and, most likely, taken away and executed.

But miraculously, as I neared the checkpoint, the officer in charge ordered that the girls should be allowed to board without being checked. I walked on board, accompanied by the other women who were going with our group. As I look back on it, it is very clear to me that God's hand was protecting me, through my mother's wisdom. I will never forget that moment, when the path of life and the path of death drew so near for me that they almost intersected.

During these troubled times, so many young people of my age—both men and women—were consumed by the bloodshed. That I escaped, not only on this occasion, but also on many other, similar ones, is, to me, a clear demonstration of God's provision for my life.

As the steamer cast off and headed out into the river, I went to a toilet and took off the girl's clothing, in great fear at every moment that my subterfuge would be discovered and I would be taken to the soldiers. After I had hidden the girl's clothes, I sat down outside the toilet, pretending to be ill. Since I was half-dead with anxiety and fear for my life, it was not difficult to pretend.

Somehow, I survived that night—one of the longest of my life. A day and half later, we docked in Malakal. Once again, my uncle Thuc Ajang welcomed me to his home. A few days later, I found one of my teachers from the school in Adong, a man named Mamuut. We used to call him "Mabil Deduer"; in the Jieng language, this means something like "The Beater." He was a devout believer in the value of physical punishment, and he vigorously applied his beliefs to the students in his charge!

Despite his rough approach to discipline, he was glad to see me, and I requested that he enroll me in Bender Primary School for Boys, where he was headmaster. I was extremely eager to continue my education, and it seemed that finally, after my harrowing escape from Bor, I was about to get the opportunity.

1. Robert O. Collins, *The Southern Sudan in Historical Perspective* (London: Transaction Publishers, 2006), 24.
2. Ibid, 1.
3. See, for example, "Cattle Raiding in Jonglei, South Sudan," available at http://www1.american.edu/ted/ICE/jonglei.html (accessed February 29, 2016).

4. Andrew S. Natsios, *Sudan, South Sudan, and Darfur: What Everyone Needs to Know* (New York: Oxford University Press, 2012), 41–45.

5. See, for example, Joseph Lagu, *The Sudan: Odyssey through a State from Ruin to Hope* (Omdurman: Omdurman Ahlia University/MOB Center for Sudanese Studies, 2006), 60.

6. Birgitta Grosskinsky and Caroline Gullick, "Exploring the Potential of Indigenous Wild Food Plants in Southern Sudan," Proceedings of a Workshop Held in Lokichoggio, Kenya, June 3–5, 1999. Published by the Mitchell Group for USAID, January 2000 (online). Available at http://pdf.usaid.gov/pdf_docs/Pnacg706.pdf; accessed May 28, 2016.

7. Edgar O'Ballance, *The Secret War in the Sudan: 1955–1972* (London: Faber and Faber, 1977), 41.

CHAPTER 2

Seeking an Education, Finding Faith

The day after I saw my former teacher, I met him at the Bender School, as he had suggested. In order to place me properly in classes, he had to assess my current level of learning. He gave me an Arabic book from the third year of study and told me to read it.

I could not. I was able to speak Arabic, as required by our northern rulers, but in the time since I had been forced to leave the school in Adong because of the war, I had forgotten most of what I had learned about how to read it. Mamuut was visibly disappointed as he informed me that, since I was unable to read Arabic at the proper level, he would not be able to enroll me in classes at his school.

I was devastated. Though I may not have been able to verbalize it at the time, I knew in the core of my being that the only path of escape for me from the cycle of violence and ignorance was to get an education. And yet, what I had hoped was a fresh opportunity had just disappeared, because of my inability to read Arabic.

Mamuut advised me to find evening classes that I could enroll in. Because of my age at this time, I would not be allowed to enter one of the more basic classes at the Bender School, he told me. I decided to find work during the day and enroll in adult education classes at night.

Soon after, I reported to the Malakal office of the Ministry of Labour, along with dozens of others who were seeking employment. As I looked up and down the queue, I realized that I was the youngest person there.

A ministry official came out and walked along the queue, choosing those he thought most fit for the work that was available that day. He walked past me twice without choosing me, so when he came by the third time, I quickly stepped forward and said to him, "Please, I want to work; add me to the people you have picked." He told me I was too young for the work that day, and that it was very hard work.

As I was trying to convince the official to add me to the work team, Mr. Daniel Deng Kut, who was the chief accountant for the local office of the Ministry of Labour, happened to be standing about ten meters away. He heard my earnest pleas with the official, and after the official left the queue and went back inside, Mr. Deng followed him to his office and told him that I should be included on the list of workers for the day. I will always be thankful that God placed me in the path of this good, Christian man; he sympathized with the plight of a desperate boy, and because of him I was able to begin making my way in life.

It was indeed hard work; we were to cut and clear grass and clean along the roadsides in Malakal. But Mr. Deng had convinced the official to include me among the workers, and he also told me to come back the next day. I was intensely grateful to him for helping me find this first opportunity to earn a living in Malakal.

The next morning, I reported as advised, and I was included on a crew that went to the home of Mr. Deng, where we cut grass and did other cleaning work. For three months, I reported each day to the roll call at the Ministry of Labour, and for three months I worked at Mr. Deng's home. At the end of that first three months, he instructed me not to go to the roll call each morning, and he also invited me to come and live with him, in a separate room within his household compound. He had a number of daughters attending the Bender School for Girls, and he gave me the responsibility of escorting them to school for the week and escorting them back home for the weekend. I came to know Akuar Mayan, Yaar Kuai, and many other girls who were students at the boarding school. I also developed a deep friendship with Daniel Deng Kut that continues to this day. In time, my own daughter would marry into the Kwaai Kut family.

I enrolled in evening classes that were offered through an outreach ministry of the United Anglican Church of Sudan and the Presbyterian Church. As I began to make progress in my education in subjects like reading, mathematics, and history, I soon realized that I was also learning about matters of infinitely greater importance.

❖ ❖ ❖

In order to understand the deep and broad influence of Christianity in South Sudan, one must consider the history of the nation and its development. Although historically the Nilotic culture practiced animist religion, Christianity has existed in some parts of the country since almost the original founding of the Church on the Day of Pentecost. Indeed, the story of the Ethiopian eunuch, found in the eighth chapter of the New Testament book of Acts, attests the presence of Christians in this part of Africa since the very earliest days.

In 1959, when plans for the Aswan Dam to be extended in height were announced, concerted efforts focused on surveying and preserving the archaeological record of ancient Nubia that would be submerged beneath the waters of the expanding lake. The many digs conducted in the region, which is mostly in northern Sudan and southern Egypt, revealed ancient churches and exquisite murals, built and crafted by Christians who lived there at least as early as the fifth century A.D. Most of the Christian culture of Nubia was swept away when Islam moved in from northern Africa, beginning in the eighth century, with the exception of Coptic Christianity, which continues to this day, especially in Ethiopia and parts of Egypt.

The Roman Catholic Church initiated mission efforts in Sudan beginning in the early 1500s. These attempts faced many difficulties, including disease, difficult terrain, and the isolation caused by great distances. Nevertheless, the Roman Catholic Church was the first Christian group after the coming of Islam to exhibit a sustained interest in establishing a presence in the southern part of the country, building a church in Gondokoro, just north of modern Juba, in 1852. They also were the first to begin training African ministers to evangelize their own people, which, though now commonly accepted as the best approach, was a revolutionary concept at the time.[1]

With the coming of the British-Egyptian Condominium in 1899, the influence of Christian churches grew even more rapidly. In many ways, this occurred as much for sociological reasons as for religious ones. Once again, we must look to history to understand why this is so.

In Islam, fellow Muslims may not be enslaved. However, prisoners of war—especially those considered infidels by the Muslim faithful—may be taken as chattel. Thus, for the Muslim traders and fighters moving into Sudan from Arabia and Egypt, there was no ethical or religious compunction against taking slaves from among the black, Nilotic, animistic people of sub-Saharan Africa—including southern Sudan.

But the coming of the British largely put an end to the Muslim slave trade in the south; at the very least, this pernicious practice was greatly curtailed by British policy. Additionally, the British allowed and, in some cases, encouraged Christian denominations to establish churches and schools in the non-Muslim south. To avoid interdenominational skirmishing, each group was given its own geographic area of concentration.

Thus, many southern Sudanese gained their first access to education because of the efforts of the Christian churches. Additionally, they came to see the British—and by extension, the churches they allowed to operate and, in some sense, protected—as a safeguard against the oppression and depredations historically visited upon the south by northern, Muslim entities. In this context, it is not difficult to understand why Christianity—and the very tangible benefits it afforded—became viewed in such a positive light by so many southern Sudanese. The Christian church in southern Sudan thus acquired, over time, a position of influence and even socio-political authority that is often surprising to persons from the West—even other Christians.

Outcomes of this historical and social phenomenon may be easily observed today in South Sudan. When, for example, an area political leader calls for a meeting or other public assembly, a few dozen of the most important or directly concerned people may attend. But let a bishop or other church leader issue a call for a gathering, and throngs of hundreds will invariably show up.[2] Similarly, when the time came in southern Sudan to communicate with the general population about the decisions around the referendum for independence that occurred in 2011, the nation's political leaders turned to the churches to take the lead in this important task of mass education and outreach. They knew that this was the only way to successfully reach the largest proportion of the population in the south; the overwhelming results of this effort proved the accuracy of their assessment.

❖ ❖ ❖

Because religious instruction was a part of the program of study at the night school I was attending, I soon began learning about the Christian faith: about its all-powerful God and especially about Jesus Christ, who, it was said, came to earth as the very representation of God in order to show mankind how to live and to provide a way to inherit eternal life. Far from resisting this teaching, I found myself drawn to it, almost overpoweringly.

As I listened to the stories from the Bible, I found much that was familiar to me. The God I met in these narratives had many similarities to Nhialic, the mighty creator of traditional Jieng religion. And in the sacrifices of the Old Testament, I could perceive the outlines of the way a village might offer up cattle in thanks for a bountiful millet harvest, how a mother might offer a chicken to insure the recovery of a sick child, or how a family might ceremonially kill an animal to bless the manhood ceremony of a son.

But in the great sacrifice, the conscious, all-encompassing act of self-giving that was the crucifixion of Jesus Christ, I saw a more amazing sacrifice than any I could ever have imagined before. And this sacrifice, I was told, was for me. The Almighty Creator himself, it was said, had, in the person of Jesus Christ, given himself up to death in order that my sins might be forgiven and I might obtain eternal life.

For a boy who never knew his father, this was an overpowering thought. The notion that I might be the object of such unfathomable love and favor on the part of the all-powerful God of heaven staggered me with its implications. Despite the danger that surrounded me, I was cared for. I was not an orphan; I was the beloved child of Almighty God. Despite having not a single cow to my name, I was esteemed as someone of very great worth! This God, I learned, had been watching over me since the moment of my birth—and even before, when I was "knit together in the secret place," as the Psalmist says. How could I possibly resist such magnificent love?

The Christian faith also provided what seemed to me logical explanations for questions I had wondered about as a boy. For example, traditional Jieng religion holds that when we die, our spirits go … somewhere. But now, in the teaching of the Bible, I understood that our spirits leave our bodies when we die, but only to await the great resurrection at the end of days, when we shall all be given new bodies, as the apostle Paul explains in chapter fifteen of the first epistle to the Corinthians, and in other places.

I entered catechism classes and eventually received baptism from Rev. Paul Adun Jok, a Presbyterian minister who was trained at Bishop Gwynne College, an institution of the Episcopal Church of Sudan. In fact, he served both Presbyterian and Episcopal congregations, due to the scarcity of qualified ministers in that part of the country at that time. Also at this time, greater unity was being sought among the various Christian denominations, which was also a reason for the unified church in Malakal that came about by the efforts of the Anglicans and other church missionary societies.

❖❖❖

Up until about 1962, a system of cooperation had arisen among several of the Christian denominations operating in southern Sudan. Missionaries from the United States and the United Kingdom conceived of a plan to bring together missionaries and ministers of various denominations in order to better facilitate the spread of the Gospel and the work of the churches in a country with almost no infrastructure or resources. Thus, the school I was attending was founded and sponsored by the Presbyterian Church in a cooperative effort with the Anglican Church in Sudan. Such interdenominational cooperation, while admirable, was also by this time a means of survival for the Christian churches in Sudan.

With the British gone in 1962, Khartoum, viewing foreign missionaries and their activities with deep suspicion, passed the Missionary Societies Act, which strictly circumscribed what foreign missionaries could and could not do in Sudan. They had previously forbidden the return to Sudan of missionaries on leave, and now they would exert even more control over the Christian activities permitted in the country. The 1962 act, for example, limited missionary activities to categories covered by a license that had to be obtained from a council of ministers that was under the control of the Khartoum government; it forbade any gathering in Christian churches except for worship and the instruction of new believers; it required any person under the age of eighteen to have the approval of a legal guardian before being baptized. The few missionaries who remained in Sudan were subject to increasing harassment and limitations.

For example, if a church required repairs, permission had to be obtained from the government before the work could begin. Of course, such permission was rarely ever granted, and was practically impossible to get. Khartoum placed many other official obstacles in the way of the Christian churches of Sudan, as I would learn first-hand, some years later.

And then, in 1964, the Khartoum government enforced the expulsion from Sudan of all foreign missionaries. Within two weeks, they were gone, and the young and struggling churches of Sudan were left on their own to face the challenges posed by a central government that was determined to assert Islam by whatever means necessary.[3] Naturally, all these measures greatly hampered efforts at evangelization—which, of course, was as the northern government intended. However, one result that they did not intend was that the oppression felt by all the churches in the south drove them together, uniting their meager resources in order to continue to exist. This unity in the face of official hostility provided the basis and foundation for the Sudan Council of Churches, which was officially inaugurated in 1965.

It is very interesting to note that at the time of the expulsion of the foreign missionaries, the Anglican Church in Sudan had some 5,000 members. Today, there are around 4.5 million Episcopal Christians in Sudan, ministered to by 45 bishops who oversee some 3,000 priests! This is a telling testimony to the power of faith, even for a repressed people.

❖ ❖ ❖

Despite all the problems facing the churches of South Sudan at that time, I became, at the age of eighteen, a baptized believer in Jesus Christ. I began my new life. The values and ethical imperatives of my new faith began to permeate my view of the world, my understanding of society, and my aims for the future. By the word of our Lord Jesus Christ, I acquired an entirely new way of thinking.

God had saved me from being an orphan and had given me a new family: people who desired my welfare, both spiritually and physically. Because I was cared for and served by faithful ministers of Christ, I became determined to prepare myself to care for and serve others. Because God was now taking care of me, I conceived a deeply felt calling to take care of others.

Clearly, these were the days when I first began to dream of being a minister of the Gospel. I also received my first experiences in leadership during this time, when I joined a Boy Scout troop sponsored by the state. The scoutmaster was Mr. Ali Daap, and under his tutelage I eventually became an assistant troop leader. In 1967, I helped lead the other boys as we traveled to a large gathering of scouts near Khartoum, at a place called Khor-Jalab.

The education I was receiving at the church-sponsored school was also equipping me to further my goals. Because I was now reading Arabic and English at the appropriate levels, as well as progressing in other subjects, I was qualified to enter a primary school from which I might receive the necessary credentials to proceed to a more advanced education. Early in 1968, I resigned from my work through the Ministry of Labour in Malakal and traveled north on the White Nile to Malut, where there was a primary school in which I could register.

I began classes in Malut and, for a time, all was well. But once again, war would interrupt my plans for getting an education. Within a few months of my arrival, because of unrest in the area related to the ongoing activities of Anya Nya, the northern army began a crackdown, arresting anyone they suspected of involvement with or sympathy toward the southern resistance movement.

Two boys of about my same age were picked up by the authorities one day, and they never returned to school. As far as any of my friends or I could tell, they had simply disappeared. It is not unlikely that they were executed, if the army suspected they were Anya Nya sympathizers—or even likely to become such. An ominous atmosphere descended on the school, especially among those of us who were deemed to be males of fighting age.

If one were snatched by the authorities, the choices were simple: either deny any involvement with Anya Nya and accept forcible recruitment into the northern army, or be taken into the bush and shot. This was the stark situation we boys faced, and these unappealing alternatives were never far from our minds or absent from our discussions.

Eventually, I came to the difficult decision that in order to save my life, I had to leave the school. I told my friend, Deng Malual Mabuor, of my conclusions, and he tried to dissuade me. Nevertheless, I had become convinced that the situation was likely to get worse before it got better. I very much feared that the next time the soldiers came to our school, they would pull me out and take me away; I could not bear the thought.

Not all young men in the south thought as I did; some decided to join Anya Nya in the fight against the Khartoum government. Because, at this time, Anya Nya relied principally on local or regional efforts,[4] some joined its ranks because they saw it as a chance to fight for their own villages, families, and clans. I suppose that they thought it was better to be actively opposing the Khartoum regime rather than passively suffering its repressive policies. Presumably, Anya Nya could offer them a purpose for living and at least a meager expectation of a means for subsistence, along with some hope for a better future for the people of southern Sudan.

But for me, this was not the way.

Make no mistake, the repressive environment created by the Khartoum government created a very fertile ground for recruitment by Anya Nya. At this time, non-Muslim Sudanese were being vigorously and purposefully marginalized. South Sudanese intellectuals were being killed or hunted into hiding. As I had already experienced, schools were often closed because of the war, and employment in southern Sudan was becoming more and more scarce, especially for non-Muslims. All of these factors combined to foster deep resentment—even hatred—of the Khartoum government among young men of my age in southern Sudan. The prospect of joining with a group that was doing something—anything—to resist the injustice was intensely appealing to many of my peers.

But I could not accept this course for myself. Many of the boys joining the fight already had more education than I. Also, I very much wanted to escape the difficult life I had known as a young boy in the bush villages, and I knew that to do this, I would need an education— impossible to achieve while traveling with a band of anti-government guerilla fighters. I even gave some thought to a deferred enlistment in the resistance movement—after I had completed at least a primary education. Indeed, I almost put this plan into action two years later, as I will relate.

At this time, though, I decided that I wanted to join Anya Nya later, after I had received my primary education. Most of my friends who had joined already had completed their basic education, but I still needed to learn to read and write.

A few days later, as all these thoughts were going through my mind, I got word of a lorry that was traveling from Malut to Khartoum. In the relative anonymity of the capital and away from the primary locations where Anya Nya was active, I thought that I might perhaps escape notice from the authorities. Bundling my meager possessions into a small pack, I climbed onto the lorry. For the three days required to travel over the rough roads, barely more than rutted tracks, that led to Khartoum, I prayed almost constantly for the preservation of my life and for a chance to begin once more—somehow—in the capital city.

The protecting hand of God was with me, however, and I finally climbed down from the lorry, coated with dust and bone-weary from the jolting journey. I was alive, I was in Khartoum, and I had another chance to seek my way forward. Despite my fatigue and all the unknowns facing me, I was thankful.

1. Andrew C. Wheeler, "Christianity in Sudan," in *Dictionary of African Christian Biography* (online); available at http://www.dacb.org/history/christianity%20in%20sudan.html (accessed March 30, 2016).
2. Andrew Natsios, former US Special Envoy to Sudan, private interview, November 25, 2015.
3. Collins, *Southern Sudan in Historical Perspective*, 69.
4. John Ryle, Justin Willis, Suliman Baldo, and Madut Jok, eds., *The Sudan Handbook* (Suffolk, UK: Boydell & Brewer, Ltd., 2011), 128.

CHAPTER 3

Escape to Khartoum

Some readers may think it very strange that, in my strong desire to find a place of safety where I could continue my education, I would actually go to the very city that was the seat of the Muslim government and the source of the harsh military repression of the people of southern Sudan. However, even here, in the seat of power for the Muslim government of the country, there were many people from southern Sudan living, working, and even practicing the Christian religion. Actually, being farther away from the locations of conflict between the southern Sudanese guerilla fighters and the government troops made me safer in Khartoum than I would have been had I stayed where I was, in Malut.

And so it was that before I had been in Khartoum very long, I was able to make contact with a group of Jieng believers from Khartoum North Evangelical Church. In fact, they maintained teams of "greeters" who kept watch at the bus and train stations, watching for people from southern Sudan who arrived in the capital and appeared to be in need of assistance. I am sure that after all my experiences and my long and difficult journey from Malut, I must have been easy for them to notice.

I also had relatives in Khartoum, and they welcomed me warmly into their home. Some of these people had left Twic East County after the terrible flooding in 1961, and I had not seen them since. I was very glad indeed to be reunited with them.

Many of my relatives had found work in the cotton factories in Khartoum, many of which were owned by Japanese companies. The Japanese had become dominant in the textile industry in Sudan, largely because of the lower import duties paid by foreign companies, a policy that started during the Condominium government of 1899–1955.[1]

My relatives urged me to apply to the factories; they assured me I could get work there very easily, since most of the factories were at that time running three full shifts. However, my priority was to be able to go to school. In order to attend night classes, I would need to finish my work in the afternoon.

After two months, I was employed by the town clerk of Khartoum North, and the office where I worked was near the young people's club that was sponsored by Khartoum North Evangelical Church. Though my salary was only twenty Sudanese pounds per month, I was finished with my job by two o'clock in the afternoon, so I had no trouble in getting to classes on time.

Dau Akech and Phillip Ajuang were among the teachers for the night classes. They were all students at the University of Khartoum, and they were offering the classes as an aid for southerners who were trying to better themselves. With their assistance, and with the faithful support of my relatives and other friends in Khartoum, I was able to complete what I had started back in Malakal. I finished four years of primary education and another four years of senior education. Finally, I was moving along the path that I hoped would lead me to a successful life.

❖ ❖ ❖

In 1971, while I was still completing my basic education in the night classes, I was appointed by the Jieng congregation as an evangelist. Gabriel Geu Anyang Jok, the principal leader of the congregation, recognized my enthusiasm for the faith and my dedication to improving my lot as important leadership qualities.

I admired him, first of all, because he was a student at the University of Khartoum, studying for his law degree. Also, I considered him to be a very capable leader, and naturally I was eager to be helpful when he asked me to assist him with teaching the people in our church. For his part, I believe that he recognized my enthusiasm for being active in the congregation.

At any rate, I was deeply honored to be recognized as worthy of the responsibility, and very soon I was deeply involved in evangelistic and outreach efforts of the church in the northern area of Khartoum.

The district of Khartoum North, or Bhari, sits at the confluence of the Blue and White Nile Rivers. Immediately across the White Nile from Khartoum North is Omdurman, the most populous metropolitan area in Sudan. Khartoum North also sits atop the city of Khartoum proper, which lies directly across an east-west bend in the Blue Nile River. Our church was active throughout all these areas, spreading the Gospel and setting up centers for Christian worship wherever believers could be found. We opened many such centers in Omdurman, Jeraf, Bhari, and many other places in the area.

But we had to be careful. The Muslim government did not support the spread of the Christian religion, and often we had to go from house to house among the southerners living in Khartoum, conducting our evangelism meetings and other activities out of the public eye. There were also many northerners who were kind and welcoming. And so, for a long time, the Muslim government was not fully aware of everything we were doing in Khartoum North and elsewhere to make Christian disciples and to strengthen their faith.

For a while, we were even allowed to organize parades and other gatherings during Christian holidays. For example, we marched through the streets at Christmas time, waving Christian flags, and we even had the government's official blessing in this, including a police escort. However, by 1970, the government position had changed, and we were no longer allowed to march. On one occasion, we took to the streets anyway, in resistance of the government order; we were met with police in riot gear who attacked us with tear gas.

It became more and more obvious to the government that the Christians of Sudan—even those of us living in Khartoum—were adamantly opposed to the official policy of Islamization and Arabization.

Despite official disapproval of our activities, we persisted in preaching and teaching wherever we could. The Christians in Khartoum built church centers in Kosti, Wad Madani, Kenana, and other towns and communities all around Khartoum. In this way, we were thwarting the government's efforts to make Sudan wholly Muslim in religion and Arabic in culture.

One of the factors that made this effort possible was the strong unity among the Sudan Council of Churches, at that time led by Joseph Maosbier, who served as Secretary General. He had a deep commitment to the Christian faith that motivated him to provide compassionate assistance to the many internally displaced persons from the south. He was a unifying leader who sought to bring all South Sudanese together within the church.

As official disapproval increased, more and more of our efforts were forced underground. These were the days when we were no longer able to march openly on Christian holidays or engage in other public activities in support of our faith. But we never stopped working to spread the Gospel and to build more church centers. At this time, I was very active in evangelistic and church leadership work in many of the rural areas south of Khartoum. Led by ministers like the late Rt. Rev. Ruben Maciir Makoi—who later became bishop of Cuibet, Lakes State—and Pastor Butrus Dingar—originally from the Nuba Mountains region in Southern Kordofan—we were teaching and baptizing thousands of people each year.

Though the Nuba Mountains are an area of Sudan that has traditionally been Muslim, many people there became believers in Christ. Ironically, Nubia was largely Christian by the end of the third century A.D., and remained so until the Kingdom of Nubia was subdued by Arab invaders, early in the sixteenth century. As previously mentioned, the intense archaeological activity in connection with the building of the Aswan High Dam revealed a widespread and vigorous Christian community that existed in the territory of the ancient Kingdom of Nubia for more than a millennium.

In more modern times, Christian evangelism in the Nuba Mountains can be traced back to at least 1935, when the Anglican Church Missionary Society established a station at Salara, in the western portion of the region.[2] Indeed, it is likely that mission activities actually preceded this, since the Sudan United Mission had been in the Nuba Mountains long enough to begin establishing its own mission stations in places like Abri, Heiban, Kauda, Moro, Talodi, and Tabanya.[3]

By the early 1970s, several active Christian communities existed in the area of Khartoum that were largely composed of Nubian believers. Perhaps because of the historical Christian origins of the Nuba people, we were able to make many new converts among them.

To my great sorrow, these believers have been suffering severe repression in recent years. In early 2014, a church in Omdurman serving believers who were mostly from the Nuba Mountains was demolished by order of the government. The Khartoum government considers these people as sympathetic to the Sudan People's Liberation Army North, which continues to fight against the repression of the Islamist northern regime, even though the SPLA-N numbers Muslims among its ranks. Our brothers and sisters who still live in the north believe sincerely that the government intends to rid the country of Christians; they live with this fear every day of their lives.

❖ ❖ ❖

During the early 1970s, when I was engaged in this evangelistic work, Anya Nya, now under the leadership of Joseph Lagu, was becoming stronger and stronger in the southern part of the country. Those of us in living in the north who sympathized with the effort to resist the government's Islamization program secretly collected money and organized groups of people to travel to the south. By 1972, the southern resistance movement had become so strong and well entrenched that the Khartoum government finally had to recognize its inability to put an end to Anya Nya and its supporters.

Having faced several serious challenges to his leadership, Jaafer Numayri, the president of Sudan who had taken power in a 1969 coup, realized that he could not secure a military victory over an enemy who was growing in strength and at the same time retain his hold on power in Khartoum amid the instability among his supposed allies. With the help of Abel Alier, a Jieng whom he had appointed Minister of Southern Affairs, Numayri began quietly discussing a political settlement with southern leaders. The leaders of the Christian churches in the south, along with representatives of the World Council of Churches and the All-Africa Conference of Churches, were also instrumental in helping the peace process to move forward.[4]

In February 1972, an accord was signed in Addis Ababa, Ethiopia, by Numayri and by Joseph Lagu, the leader of Anya Nya, that effectively ended the First Sudanese Civil War, after seventeen long years of violence and bloodshed. The terms of this agreement granted autonomy—though not complete independence—to southern Sudan, creating the Southern Sudan Autonomous Region. With the signing of this agreement and the end of the war, widespread rejoicing broke out among southerners, both Christian and those following traditional religions.

Many southerners who had moved north to escape the violence went back to their homes in the south, taking their newfound Christian faith with them. It was a time of intense spiritual revival: hundreds of new churches were established, especially in Jonglei State; believers were composing new hymns and translating others into their native tongues; scores of people were coming to faith; more and more people were hearing the Gospel preached, and then preaching it to others.

I led a team that included Bishop Nathaniel Garang, the late Abraham Agot, and Lazarus Garang Bul. These faithful brothers and I walked the territory from Chuiker to Duk Padiet—a distance of almost 200 miles— in order to preach the Christian faith to as many people as possible.

Because of the work we had been doing to spread the Gospel in the north, very few of the southerners who came to the north converted to

Islam. Furthermore, we gained many converts to the Christian faith from among those who had previously been Muslim. The full extent of our success did not become immediately apparent, but as the true situation became clear, those in power became more and more displeased and also more determined to halt the spread of our faith. Some years later, this deep mistrust of Christianity on the part of the Muslim government would result in the repressive September Laws of 1983, edicts that would do much to precipitate the tragic and bloody Second Sudanese Civil War.

In 1975, the Jieng congregation I was working with in Khartoum asked several of us to take the entrance examination for a deacon's training curriculum that was to be offered in Mundri, far to the south. Two of us scored the necessary grade on the exam: Butrus Kwo—who would eventually become a bishop in the Diocese of Port Sudan—and myself. In July, we boarded a steamer and made our way south to Juba, where we were welcomed by Rev. Canon Clement Janda, then provincial secretary for the church. The next day we got in a truck bound for Mundri, almost 125 miles northwest of Juba. Mundri was at that time the home of Bishop Gwynne College, where we would pursue our studies.

Unfortunately, the truck broke down in a place called Lui, about fifteen miles short of our destination. It was about three o'clock in the afternoon when this happened. Unlike today, when we could have simply made a call on a mobile phone, we had no way to alert the staff of the college of our whereabouts or our predicament.

We were then in the middle of the rainy season, and fifteen miles of dense jungle lay between Lui and Mundri. Because Butrus Kwo had his wife and children with him, I told him to stay with the truck, and I would walk the remaining fifteen miles to Mundri to inform the people at the college about what had happened, so that they could perhaps send a vehicle to pick everyone up and bring them safely to Mundri.

Of course, I was not familiar with the countryside in Equatoria, the state where Mundri is located. In fact, it was the first time I had ever been there. I must admit that I was a bit nervous as I walked alone through the forest, listening every moment for any sound that might be the warning of a threat to my safety. I was not too worried about human attackers, but the area was home to leopards, hyenas, and lions, any of which could, under the right circumstances, pose great danger to a single individual traveling on foot. The walk took two hours, and it was certainly not a peaceful stroll for me.

However, at about 6:00 p.m. I arrived safely in Mundri and found my way to Bishop Gwynne College. Rev. Eluzai Monda, the principal of the school, greeted me, though he was, of course, puzzled that I was not only alone, but also on foot. I told him what had happened to the truck, and he said that since it was already dark, he would wait until morning to send a car for Butrus Kwo, his family, and everyone else who was with the truck in Lui. A few years later, Eluzai Monda would be consecrated as Bishop of Mundri and Dean of that province of the Episcopal Church of Sudan.

Though I was concerned about my friend and his family having to spend the night in a truck in the jungle, I was certainly relieved and happy to be at Bishop Gwynne College. I was about to take the next major step in my journey as I gained the knowledge needed to become an ordained leader in the Episcopal Church of Sudan.

1. David E. Mills, *Dividing the Nile: Egypt's Economic Nationalists in the Sudan, 1918-56* (Cairo: The American University Press in Cairo, 2014), 192–202.
2. Justin Willis, "The Nyamang Are Hard to Touch": Mission Evangelism and Tradition in the Nuba Mountains, Sudan, 1933–1952. In *Journal of Religion in Africa*, 33(1), February 2003, 32–62.
3. Centre for the Study of Christianity in the Non-Western World, "African Missions, Education, and the Road to Independence: The SUM in Nigerian, The Cameroons, Chad, Sudan, and Other African Territories" [online]. Available at http://www.ampltd.co.uk/digital_guides/african_missions_parts_1_to_3/Publishers-Note.aspx (accessed August 31, 2016).
4. Andrew Natsios, *Sudan, South Sudan, and Darfur*, 76.

CHAPTER 4

Revival in South Sudan

Bishop Gwynne College, named after Llewellyn Gwynne, the pioneer missionary of the Anglican Church in Sudan, is one of the most deeply respected institutions of higher learning in all of South Sudan. In its more than seventy years of existence, it has trained most of the principal ministers and leaders of the Episcopal Church of Sudan.

The college had its beginnings as the Yei Divinity School in 1945, started by a young missionary named Fred Crabb. But its location in Yei, far in the south, near the border with the Congo, was not very ideal for the people of southern Sudan. Thus, in 1947 the campus was moved about 90 miles north, to Mundri, and was renamed in honor of Bishop Gwynne. Crabb and his wife had to leave Sudan in 1951 due to ill health, and from 1954 to 1961 David Brown became the principal, carrying on Crabb's vision. Brown dubbed Bishop Gwynne College "the village of God." During his tenure, BGC served not only the Anglican fellowship but also the American Mission of the Presbyterian Church of North America and the Sudan United Mission, later called Sudan Interior Church. The first Sudanese to head BGC was Rev. Samuel Jangul. Rev. Paul Aduljok represented the American Mission, and others came later.[1]

By the time I got there in the summer of 1975, the campus had suffered severe neglect during the many years of the first civil war. It had been closed since 1964 because of the violence throughout southern Sudan, and the buildings that had not actually been destroyed by the fighting were in very poor repair. Trees and elephant grass had overgrown the campus so that it was difficult to even notice the buildings, in some cases. For the first three months of my occupancy at the college, I, along with my fellow students, spent most of my time clearing elephant grass and cutting back the trees in order to make the campus more useable.

The food at the college was another challenge I faced. Remember, I had just come from Khartoum, the national capital, and I was accustomed to buying bread in a store and having access to other delicacies that are available in a large city environment. But at Mundri, in a much more remote location, we had only the vegetables and other foods that could be obtained nearby or by gathering in the surrounding forest. The local women who were assigned the task of finding and preparing our food were very good at their job, but despite their efforts, I often felt as if I would never again have enough to eat.

I was also the youngest student in the class of ten, and one of only three who were unmarried. At times, this caused me to feel rather lonely.

But despite all these things, I was very pleased to be engaged in study and learning. I also believe that the many difficult experiences of my earlier life had trained me to remain patient, to be self-reliant, and above all, to persevere. I knew that the training and education I would receive at BGC would be invaluable for me, and I sincerely believed that I was there due to God's grace and because of his calling.

❖ ❖ ❖

I was assigned living quarters in a barracks that was in use by a battalion of Anya Nya soldiers, most of whom were from Aweil, in Bahr el Ghazal. Few of them were Christians. I decided that these men were my mission field at that time. For the three years I was at the college, I continued to speak to them about the Gospel and to teach as many of them as I could about the Bible. Over time, the atmosphere in the barracks became much more compatible with the Christian way of life, as many of the soldiers and their families were baptized. Rev. Manasseh Banyi Daudi, the dean of students for the college, baptized many of them. Later, Rev. Daudi was consecrated as the bishop of Kajo-keji Diocese. Over my three years in BGC, I trained four of my barracks mates to become evangelists. At the end of my studies, we parted ways. Imagine my delight, when, forty years later, I was reunited with Daniel Amat, whom I met in the barracks while at Bishop Gwynne College. In they years since, he had become an evangelist and was still very active in the Christian faith.

I was also active with the youth of the Moru tribe, which lives in the area of Mundri. I helped to organize the Moru Youth Leadership group; the first appointed leader was Juslin Nura. Later, she was married to Roja Chalen, the son of a missionary among the Jieng people of Akot, a town almost in the center of southern Sudan, in what is now called Lakes State.

The ten students in my class were myself and Butrus Kwa, from the Diocese of Khartoum; Kenneth Barioga and Joseph Philip, from the Diocese of Mundri; Nelson Nyumba and Criton Anguora, from the Diocese of Kajo-keji; Eluzai Michael and Elisa Kasinga, from the Diocese of Yambio; Stephen Adwok, from the Diocese of Malakal; and Gabriel Gak, from the Diocese of Rumbek. As you can see, we were from all over the country. We all worked very hard and were dedicated to our studies. Not surprisingly, several of us came to occupy positions of leadership, both in our communities and also in the Episcopal Church of Sudan.

The college had a policy that each student should take responsibility for a small plot of land near the student's living quarters. Accordingly, I became very skilled at growing tomatoes. As a matter of fact, I was successful enough that I usually had tomatoes to offer for sale; I made pretty good money from my crops while I was a student at Bishop Gwynne! With that money, I was able to buy some cattle, a purchase that would be quite significant in my life, not too many years hence. Not only that, but my success as a tomato grower instilled in me a lifelong enjoyment for gardening and horticultural work. In all the years since these student days, I have always made sure I had some place for a garden.

During holiday breaks, when I would go back to Khartoum, I worked to organize the Jieng youth for church work and evangelism, especially in Jonglei State and, later, in Bahr-El-Ghazal. The young people in Khartoum would collect money for their efforts and then travel south to Juba. From there, we would go out to places like Bor for evangelistic activities.

The priest in charge of Bor Parish was Rev. Nathaniel Garang Anyieth; in later years he would be appointed Bishop of Bor Diocese. With the approximately fourteen young people in my group, I organized and carried out evangelistic outreach in places like Cui-keer, Kolnyang, Anyiethdit, Makuac, and Baydit. With these dedicated young people, we walked from Duken to Pawal Wangkulei, Paleu, and Maar in 1976 and 1977. We covered a large section of southern Jonglei State during this time.

As we went from village to village, we always did our best to train people who could continue evangelizing after we left. In the earliest years of European missions in Sudan, this aspect—raising up indigenous church leaders—was too often neglected. The result was that Sudanese churches remained dependent on outside "experts" for doctrinal instruction, ministry training, and church governance. As we evangelized Jonglei State, we did everything in our power to avoid this. Many of these leaders we trained went on to be strong Christian pastors and ministers for many years: Samuel Majok Deng in Duk Padiet, Mary Achol Deng in Duk Payuel, Joseph Akol Gak in Pawal and later in Duk Padiet, and many others.

Similarly, in Bor South we trained students who were committed to leading church centers and doing evangelistic work. In Bor South, we had the advantage of being able to work with students of the government schools operating there at that time.

❖❖❖

As we worked in Duk Padiet, a medium-sized town in what was then Duk County, almost in the center of Jonglei State, one of our new converts approached us with a challenging request. His name was Chuol Ayii, and he was previously a priest of the traditional African religion. He told us that he was accepting Christ, but, he said, "Now that you are leaving us, we have no one who can read the Bible you are carrying. We do not know how to write. We may remember what you told us for a week, but soon we will forget. And when the Padiet returns, it will kill us. Will you not be responsible for our deaths?"

The Bible to which he was referring was in the Jieng language, and "the Padiet" refers to a local animist religion, much like voodoo. He had posed a very difficult and important question, and the next morning we all met together to consider the best response. After much discussion and prayer, we decided to leave behind Samuel Majok Deng as an evangelist and minister for the new Christians of Duk Padiet. Samuel would later be ordained as a priest. This is the same procedure that the apostle Paul recommended to his young apprentices Timothy and Titus, when he said, "… appoint elders in every town" (Titus 1:5). We wanted to make certain that we left these very young Christians with the resources they needed to continue to grow in their faith. This included making sure that they had leaders with them who could continue to guide them in their understanding of the Gospel and the Christian faith.

As we agreed to leave Samuel in Duk Padiet, we also charged these new believers with providing for his support. They promised to build a house for him and to share their food. The youth office under my leadership committed to paying three Sudanese pounds per month for his salary, which at that time was a considerable amount of money. Similarly, in Duk Payuel we stationed Joseph Akol Gak.

Perhaps because of all these activities that I organized, I was recognized as the evangelism coordinator for all of Jonglei State. My duty was to make sure that the work we had carried out took root and flourished. I was very pleased to do this, since nothing was more important to me at the time. I was still a student at Bishop Gwynne College and the only theological student on the team, but I was coming to realize that my life's calling lay in ministering to the Christians of Sudan and in spreading the Gospel throughout my country.

However, not all my superiors were as pleased with my evangelistic work as I was. The diocesan bishop of Malakal, Kedhehia Mabior, who was previously archdeacon of Jonglei State, was concerned that because of the youth of my team, and perhaps because they all came from the Jieng communities of Khartoum, they would not be responsive to diocesan leadership. However, we had the support of Nathaniel Garang Anyeith, the parish priest for Bor, who agreed to work with us and oversee our evangelism activities.

❖ ❖ ❖

During the work in Jonglei, many people placed their faith in Christ and were baptized. All this required a great deal of commitment and energy, especially since I was also engaged in my three-year course of study for the diaconate at Bishop Gwynne College during the same period. And I was also working to mobilize the students of Juba Commercial Secondary School for evangelism in the administrative capital of southern Sudan. With the leadership of Lazarus Garang Bul, Abraham Agot, and Mabior Arok Amou, these students began to reach out more and more in Juba. In the evenings, they went to different church centers near Juba Mission, Gabat, and the school behind the Church Missionary Society (CMS). I recall that in the Thongping community, a church used to meet under a large tree; this was one of the groups that the student in Juba worked with.

As they went among the church groups, the students taught Bible lessons in English and Jieng. Many people in the Jieng communities of Juba came to Christ during this time. These were days of great celebration in Juba, due to the recent signing of the Addis Ababa Accords, and we took this as an opportunity to organize parades and revival marches and processions through the streets of Juba during the seasons of Easter, Christmas, and other Christian holidays. All this created a great interest in the church and drew many people to hear our teaching and preaching.

In 1977, as I was finishing my course of study at Bishop Gwynne College, Eluzai Monda, the principal, recommended to Butrus Tia Shukai, at that time diocesan bishop of Omdurman (later changed to the Diocese of Khartoum) that I should be ordained as a deacon. And so, in March 1977 I received my ordination, after which I returned to BGC to complete my studies. In 1978, following the end of my coursework, I was posted to Khartoum to serve the Jieng community there as a priest. At the end of that year, Bishop Shukai transferred me to Port Sudan Parish.

However, I had a very important request of the bishop before I completed my move to Port Sudan. I asked him for permission, before beginning my service in Port Sudan, to go back to the southern part of the country to make plans and arrangements for my marriage.

1. Roland Werner, William Anderson, and Andrew Wheeler, *Day of Devastation, Day of Contentment: The History of the Sudanese Church across 2,000 Years* (Nairobi: Pauline Publications, 2000), 360.

Archbishop Daniel Deng Bul Yak

Archbishop Deng and his wife, Mama Deborah Abuk Atem Mading

St. Matthew Cathedral in Renk, completed in 2006 through the generosity of many in Africa, the United States, and the United Kingdom, and also through the courage of the Christians in Renk Diocese.

Archbishop Deng, following his enthronement and consecration at All Saint's Cathedral, Juba, April 20, 2008

Archbishop Deng (2nd from right) and other church leaders, meeting with Grand Imam of Cairo's al-Azhar Mosque, Sheikh Ahmed Mohamed al Tayeb

Presidential Committee for Community Peace, Reconciliation, and Tolerance in Jonglei State, 2012. This photograph was taken at the committee's presentation to President Salva Kiir of the results from the all-Jonglei Peace Conference in 2012.

Archbishop Deng meets with UN Secretary General Ban Ki-Moon, New York, October 11, 2010

Sudanese Ecumenical Advocacy Delegation meets with UN Secretary General Ban Ki-Moon, October 11, 2010. Left to right: John Ashworth, Rev. Ramadan Chan, Most Rev. Dr. Daniel Deng Bul Yak, Ban Ki-Moon, Rt. Rev. Paride Taban, Rt. Rev. Daniel Adwok

Archbishop Deng (4th from left) with other Anglican primates, meeting with Coptic Orthodox Pope Tawadros II in Cairo

Archbishop of Canterbury Justin Welby in Bor, South Sudan, January 31, 2014

Archbishop Daniel Deng Bul Yak (center) with President Salva Kiir (left), Vice President Riak Machar (right), and Roman Catholic Bishop Poalino (center, with back to camera), praying during the signing of the peace accord, May 9, 2014, Addis Abbaba, Ethiopia

Archbishop Deng (back to camera, center) visits the young men at one of the cattle camps near Rumbek, in Lakes State, South Sudan, during a "peace mobilization" campaign in 2015.

Archbishop Deng addresses Kenyan South Sudanese diaspora, Nakuru, Kenya, February–March 2015

CHAPTER 5

Marriage and the Beginning of Ministry in Port Sudan

During the time I was working with the youth in Khartoum and Juba and organizing them for evangelism and ministry, I chanced to meet a young woman named Deborah Abuk Atem. She was very active in the church, and over time, I realized I was thinking of her more and more. Eventually, I had to admit to myself that I was quite smitten with this beautiful and charming Christian woman.

I needed two years to work my courage up to the point of being able to call on her. I talked to some trusted friends, telling them of my feelings. With their help, I got a message to her that Evangelist Daniel wished to pay her a visit.

She was surprised by this news. During all the time I had been watching and admiring her, I had done my very best to keep my feelings to myself and not to give out any signals of my growing interest in her. When she received my formal request for an appointment, she felt quite nonplussed. And then, as the time for the meeting neared, she became suspicious.

On the day agreed upon, about 5:00 p.m., I went to her house with my friends Lazarus Garang Bul, Abraham Agot, and several other young people who were often in my company. In the meantime, Deborah had also invited a number of her friends to be present. Thus, when I arrived at her house with my entourage in tow, and she met us with her own assembly, we made a rather large gathering.

As I stood there with my friends watching me—and with her friends watching me, too—I was at a loss for what to say. With so many eyes watching, it did not seem the right time to speak in flowery words of my feelings for Miss Atem. On the other hand, I was the one who had asked for this meeting to be arranged. I had to say something … but what?

I turned to Abraham Agot and asked him to lead us all in a word of prayer, which he did. This seemed to help; after he concluded the prayer I felt able to introduce myself to Deborah and her friends. I then introduced my friends.

Mind you, the usual Jieng way for such matters is to conduct meetings one-on-one. But as evangelist and youth leader, I felt that it was very important to do things openly and honestly, in front of witnesses. Not only did I intend for my intentions to be above suspicion, but I also wanted to set a good example for the other young people. I felt then, and I still believe today, that it is of ultimate importance for ministers of the Gospel to be open and transparent in their dealings, actions, and communications. While it is true that my motives were noble and above-board, I must also admit that this was not the easiest way one might begin a courtship!

Nevertheless, I pressed ahead. In front of the group, I told Deborah that it was my purpose to seek her hand in marriage.

A long silence greeted this pronouncement. And then, as Abraham Agot had done for me, Anna Alual Atem, Deborah's sister, graciously stepped into the breach. She thanked me for my words and also offered her gratitude to all the friends who had come with me. She said that my words had been heard and understood, but that Deborah could not give her answer, right then and there. She asked for some time for her sister to consider the proposal and give a response.

Now it was my turn, once again, to stand silent and tongue-tied. Another friend of mine, Lazarus Garang Bul, came to my aid, thanking Anna for her words and for the warm welcome we had received. After that, someone led another prayer. To this day, I cannot remember who that was, because I was still in shock.

We all parted amicably, however, and I had accomplished my principal objective: to inform Deborah Abuk Atem of my hope to take her as my wife. With that done, we proceeded to meet as occasion permitted, and to get to know each other better. But it would still be a full year before Deborah—and her sister—fully accepted me.

During that year, we spent a lot of time getting to know one another. I should explain that in Jieng culture, and especially because I was a leader in the church, it would have been very inappropriate for Deborah to spend long periods of time alone with me. This meant that when we were together, we were almost always with a group of people, whether family or friends. As you can imagine, this type of setting does not lend itself to the sort of very intimate conversations that might seem normal to young couples in the West.

Sometimes Deborah's sister was with her, and when I could, I would speak very earnestly to her sister to convince her that I was the right man for Deborah. The only times Deborah and I could be alone together were for brief moments when I was paying a formal visit to her family in their home.

Still, we did talk a lot about what our future home might be like. Naturally, we were worried that her parents might not accept me, since her father required a large dowry for her, and I did not have the cattle to pay it. But together we asked God to help us, and in our prayers together during my visits to her family, we would always beseech God that we might get married.

My friends would advise me to not give up and to maintain hope for a future with Deborah as my wife. They advised me not to worry too much about the dowry, assuring me that God would provide. They told me I should not be overly concerned about my lack of material wealth— such as cattle for a dowry or a home for the two of us to live in.

Finally, Deborah indicated that I might approach her parents to ask for her hand. And so, it was time to take the next step. As matters would prove, this part of the process would not be any easier than the first had been.

The first thing I had to do was to speak with my older brother, Malual. Since he was the oldest male in my immediate family, he would be the one whom custom would demand would make the initial approach to Deborah's father and other relatives. He was reluctant, for the reason that we did not have enough cattle for the dowry. However, I insisted that it would be better to make the request anyway and find out what sort of reply we might receive.

My brother was unmoved, so I went to our relatives to explain my predicament and make my case. I called a family meeting at which both I and my brother presented our viewpoints on the matter. My brother's position was simple: We had insufficient cattle, and the clan of my intended bride was known for driving hard bargains. They would want many cows, and we had no cows to offer. For my part, I insisted that all I wanted was for my relatives to make a visit to Deborah's parents and present my proposal to them. It would then be up to her family to accept or reject my proposal.

In the end, they agreed to do as I asked. I had carried the day with my family, but I cannot say that I felt very hopeful. As my brother and I walked away from the meeting with our relatives, I prayed as intensely as I have ever prayed about anything in my life. Clearly, I needed a miracle!

❖ ❖ ❖

We went to Pawel, the village of Deborah's family, which was about nine miles from our village. When we arrived, we sent word that we wished to meet with Isaiah Atem Mading, Deborah's father. Coincidentally, Mr. Mading had become a Christian and received baptism during the evangelism campaign I had organized in 1977.

At about 2:00 in the afternoon, my brother and I were called to meet with Deborah's father, some of the elders of the village, and a number of Deborah's uncles, including Mr. Garang Agot and Mr. Atem Deng-Thij. I had met several of these men previously, during the course of my evangelistic work in the area. But now we were meeting under different circumstances and for a very different purpose!

My brother introduced us both and explained to them why we were there. He told them of my interest in Deborah and my desire to take her as my wife. He then proceeded to inform them that he had discouraged me in this purpose, because our family was poor and we had no cows for a dowry. "We are unable to make the agreement for the marriage," he told them, "since we don't have cattle. But if God provides cattle for us in the future, we can come back and make this request again, if your daughter is not already married by that time." This was not the persuasive case I had wished to make in order to claim my beloved Deborah, but at least my brother presented the truth of the situation as it existed at that time.

After my brother finished speaking, Garang de Agot, one of Deborah's uncles, offered words of welcome and thanked us for our visit. He asked us to leave for a while so that they could consider their decision and give us a reply. My brother and I left the men of Deborah's family to their deliberations.

To me, it seemed that the family discussion went on for much longer than the hour and a half it actually lasted. I prayed fervently for the entire time, asking God for his favor and acceptance as I begged him to intervene with Deborah's family on my behalf.

At last they came out to my brother and me and asked us to come back inside. They told me that after serious debate, the decision of the majority was that I should be permitted to marry Deborah. There had been strong opinions on both sides, as I would learn later. Some of them had accepted me, while others disagreed with the idea of marrying a promising young woman like Deborah to a man who had no cows. Nevertheless, others insisted that I was strong and of good character; I would bring cows later, they said, when I had had a better chance to make my way in the world.

Perhaps the outcome was due to the impression I had made as an evangelist, or perhaps it was due to something else. But for whatever reason, Deborah's father decided to abide by the majority opinion. He told me that I could marry his daughter, with or without the customary dowry. I felt relief and joy flooding my heart, and I inwardly praised God with all my might.

❖ ❖ ❖

As my brother and I walked away from the meeting, I could tell that he was not happy with the outcome. Perhaps he thought that Deborah's family would refuse me outright, since we had no cattle to offer. He would not speak to me as we went back home.

The next day, my family had a meeting. Our relatives gathered, and they asked me to tell them all that had transpired with Deborah's family. I shared everything that had happened, and then I told them that I had five cows, which I had acquired with the money I had made from selling my tomatoes, among other things. I said that I would give these cows to Deborah's family, with the promise of an additional six cows, as soon as I was able to acquire them.

I hoped that my uncles would assist me in gathering some cattle for Deborah's dowry, but to my great disappointment, they made no offers. When my brother was asked if he could help, he also declined. Despite my displeasure at this information, I assured my family that I would go ahead, since the family of my beloved Deborah had already told me they would accept my offer of marriage.

I delivered my five cows to Deborah's family, and they accepted them graciously. They also told me that she was in Juba, and that I should go there and bring her back to her family.

❖ ❖ ❖

After a full day of walking from Pawel, I reached Bor. I traveled by river boat for another day to get to Juba, where I went to Deborah and informed her of her father's summons. The next day, we boarded a boat and traveled up the White Nile to Bor. We rested there overnight and began walking to Pawel the next morning. Though I had made the journey from her village to Bor in a single day, I found that we could not travel as fast together as I had alone. Perhaps the reason I traveled so fast on my way to Juba had something to do with my desire to see Deborah again!

As we walked along the road through the forest, nearing the village of Paliau, which is about halfway between Bor and Pawel, we saw ahead of us a very large snake. The snake, probably a red spitting cobra, proved to be very aggressive, and rather than slithering away into the bush, it came toward us. It appeared to be getting ready to attack.

As Deborah hid behind me, I picked up a stick, thinking that perhaps I could throw it at the snake and frighten it away. But then, it occurred to me that throwing the stick would leave me defenseless, and the cobra could probably move faster than we could run. I looked around for some other weapon, and I saw some large clods of dried mud. I picked up one of them in both hands as the snake got closer and closer.

I knew that cobras usually raise their heads and the front part of their bodies off the ground before they strike, hissing and showing the characteristic hood in a threat display. I waited until the snake got close enough, and when it raised its head, I slammed the clod on it as hard as I could. The snake was stunned, so I struck it again with a clod, and at that, it crawled away.

I turned around to make sure that Deborah was all right, and she had moved back a considerable distance. Possibly, her confidence in my ability to deliver her from danger was getting less as the snake got closer. I called to her and told her that the snake was gone, and we continued on our way.

We spent that night in Paliau and reached Pawel the next day, where Deborah was reunited with her family. Her father thanked me for bringing his daughter back to him, and I left for Powooi, my home village, after Deborah's father requested that I return in two days for the ceremony in which he would officially transfer the responsibility for Deborah from himself to me, as her husband.

Two days later, in the evening, I was again in Pawooi at the home of Deborah's family, together with my elder brother Malual and others. There were not many people present, but it was for me a deeply meaningful event; I was joining my life with that of my beloved. I was happier than I had ever been up until this time.

The ceremony was actually rather short. Deborah's father gave a brief speech that signified his handing over of his daughter to me, saying that we should take care of each other. He encouraged us by saying that God would bless us with children, and that the dowry issue should not worry me. "When God blesses you, I know you will take care of this and your family." My older brother thanked him and all the relatives who were gathered at the ceremony for suspending the matter of the dowry until a later time.

Deborah and I then walked back to Pawooi. Heavy rains had fallen, and because of the water standing all about, the mosquitos were unusually troublesome. We had to sleep under nets if we were to sleep at all, and when we left to go back to Bor, the countryside was so flooded that we walked in water for most of the two days required to make the journey. From Bor, we boarded a steamer that took us back to Juba, where Deborah would stay until she joined me at my new ministry assignment in the north, which at that time was in Khartoum.

❖ ❖ ❖

By this time it was October 1978. After reluctantly taking my leave from my wife, I went back to Khartoum, only to be told by the diocesan bishop that I would soon be transferred to Port Sudan Parish to serve as a priest. Archdeacon Bulus Idris accompanied me from Khartoum to Port Sudan and introduced me to the parish leaders there. Simon Nyika— now deceased—was the current pastor whom I would be replacing, and Meshach Makuei Deng was on the parish council. At that time, Deng was faithfully serving the church as a lay reader and also working at his job as head of the laboratory at one of the refineries in Port Sudan. He was the only one in the church who owned an automobile, and it became the de facto church car, used for conducting parish business and transporting church guests and officials. Of course, he was doing all this at his own expense.

Four days later, Archdeacon Idris and I returned to Khartoum. A few years later, Bulus Idris would become bishop of Khartoum Diocese, following the death of Bishop Butrus Tia Shukai in 1985.

I celebrated a rather lonely Christmas in Khartoum that year, because my dear Deborah was still in Juba. After Christmas, however, I requested that the bishop allow me to go to Kosti to welcome my wife, who would be arriving there on a steamer from Juba. With three days' leave granted, I joyfully greeted Deborah in Kosti, and we rode the bus back to Khartoum. A week later, we traveled by train to Port Sudan and the beginning of my duties as parish priest. We arrived there on January 9, 1979.

I requested of Bishop Butrus Tia Shukai that he come to Port Sudan and conduct our official church wedding. This he did, about two weeks after our arrival. It was one of the last sacraments over which this good man presided before his death, not long afterwards.

My beloved Deborah and I have, at this writing, been married for more than thirty-five years. God has richly blessed us with six wonderful children: Grace, Martha, Peter, Emmanuel, Awaak, and Isaac. At the time of our wedding, I was able to pay an additional six cows to her family. It was my intention to pay even more cows, but not long after this, war again erupted, cutting off our communications with the south and making such a transaction not only difficult, but also dangerous. Still, with the cessation of hostilities between the north and south that came in 2005, I provided thirty more cows to her family, though her parents were both deceased by that time.

Indeed, even if the total had been three hundred cows, it would still not reflect even a tenth of the value of this godly woman or the joy she has brought into my life.

CHAPTER 6

Port Sudan Parish, 1979–1994

Sudan's original port on the Red Sea was the city of Suakin, which likely served the vessels of classical Greece and the Roman empire, starting from at least the time of the Ptolemies in Egypt. Its first mention in Arab history was in the tenth century A.D., when al-Hamdani refers to it as "an ancient town." By the sixteenth century, when Portuguese mariners had discovered alternate trade routes, Suakin began to decline in importance. Today, it is a relatively small city of only about 50,000 inhabitatants.

In 1905, construction began on Port Sudan, about thirty miles up the coast from Suakin. The harbor at Suakin was choked with coral, and the British and others decided that Sudan needed a port that could more easily accommodate the modern vessels of the time. From its completion in 1909 until today, Port Sudan has received the vast majority of imports to Sudan and South Sudan. The busy docks, refineries, oil pipeline terminal, shipyards, and other industries there provide opportunities for employment to many Sudanese. With a population of almost a half million persons, Port Sudan is also the capital of Red Sea State in Sudan.

Port Sudan Parish was founded by the Episcopal Church of Sudan in 1930 as a means of outreach to the many sailors, dock workers, and other laborers living in the bustling port city. For many decades, European priests, mostly British, served the church Port Sudan. Upon my assumption of duties, I became the third Sudanese priest to serve the parish. The first was Bishop Michael Lugar, who came from east Africa at the request of Bishop Olive Alson. Following Bishop Lugar was Rev. Simon Nyika, whom I was replacing.

I must admit that I did not find a thriving church upon my arrival in Port Sudan. On the first Sunday I was there, only nine people came for worship. Ironically, the building for the church was very large, so the group of us who were gathered there looked even smaller.

The mood among the believers was not at all energetic; in fact, it was rather dull and passive. No programs existed, and there was no evangelistic or ministry work underway. In the building itself, trash and other refuse was piled about, and there was an overwhelming stench from the accumulation of pigeon droppings. The place appeared to be falling into ruin.

I immediately organized a visitation plan, and I enlisted the help of Lay Reader Meciek Makuei Deng, since he was the only person I knew in the church in Port Sudan who owned a car. He agreed to take me first to the homes of the southern Sudanese who were living in Port Sudan. I also embarked on an effort to visit all the Nubian communities in the city, which I did over a period of about two years. Many of these good people became Christians.

Before long, with encouragement and plenty of follow-up, more and more people began to come to church. Starting with the southern Sudanese and the Nubians, our attendance grew from the nine who had come that first Sunday. Soon we were having no fewer than 400 in attendance, and often the group that gathered for worship was close to 1,000 persons.

With this renewed interest kindled among the Christians of Port Sudan, we soon began evangelistic outreach efforts. As the number of believers began to increase, we opened new parishes in the city: Duam Nuur, Salalab, and High Phillip. Other, smaller Christian centers were established in the surrounding area, including Kassala, New Halpha, Gadarif, and Pau. Most of the people in these areas were southerners, though many were not part of any of the tribes that make up the majority of the population of southern Sudan. But as their priest, it was my duty to serve them, because the Gospel is for everyone of every tribe and nation, and as the New Testament teaches, God is not a respecter of persons (Acts 10:34).

The army barracks in Gebet became the site of a new church. Evangelist Mark Pajak served in this place, which also hosted a military training school for all of the Sudanese Army. Even more amazing, we planted a church inside the prison located in the old port city of Suaka, in addition to one that we established in the prison at Port Sudan.

We trained many evangelists among the people of Port Sudan, and a large number of them are still serving the church today, especially in the Nuba Mountains. And even today, Port Sudan still produces distinguished, faithful leaders for the Episcopal Church of Sudan. Bishop Saman Frajalla, Rev. Mark Fajak Avujal, Rev. Abraham Noon Jiel, and many other great servants of God, some of whom have gone on to be with the Lord, have come from this place.

❖ ❖ ❖

Mind you, doing the work of the Gospel in Port Sudan was not easy. Remember that this city is in the north of the country, an area that is predominantly Muslim. Not only did the laws favor persons of the Islamic faith (as they do even more today in Sudan), but there was and remains immense social pressure on anyone in the north who is not Muslim to convert to Islam. And for anyone who converts from Islam to Christianity or any other faith, Sharia law prescribes death as a possible penalty. While it is true that in modern times—at least, officially—this penalty is not often carried out, the social stigma attached to leaving Islam is a constant, hovering threat for many who might otherwise want to become Christians.

Not long after I arrived in Port Sudan, I faced a very practical instance of the bias against non-Muslims, involving a piece of real estate legally owned by the church. Actually, I inherited this ongoing conflict from my predecessor, Rev. Simon Nyika.

Within the church compound stood a wooden building that had fallen into disuse, likely because of the very small number of Christians who were still coming to the church prior to my arrival. The church had agreed to lease this building to the Mamshet Company, which was a clearing agent for goods in the port. Mamshet was owned by a man named Said Ahmand who also happened to be a police commander. The company used the wooden building for storage of goods in transit from or to the port.

Because of the rapid growth of the church, we soon had need of the building, so we requested that Mamshet remove its property from the building so that we could prepare it for use by the church. We also notified them that we would not renew their lease, giving them three months' notice, as required by the terms of the lease they had signed.

However, the company refused to vacate our building. When we called meetings to discuss the matter, their representatives refused to attend. They continued to send rent checks to the church, and we returned the checks to them, uncashed. For perhaps six months, the church and Mamshet enacted a kind of bizarre ritual through the mails; they would send us a check, and we would return it to them, whereupon they would re-send it, and we would once again send it back to them.

After this pointless exercise had continued for some time, we made the decision to take Mamshet to court in order to force them to vacate our premises. One of the church's neighbors was an attorney and a friend, so I went to him to get advice on the best way to proceed with our lawsuit. He listened to me carefully, and when I had told him the whole story and named Said Ahmand, the owner of Mamshet, as our adversary, he began laughing.

"I know this man," he said. "In fact, he is a friend of mine." He told me that, while he did not want to involve himself directly and thus risk a friendship on one side or the other, he would help me with the case and tell me how to proceed.

The first piece of advice he gave me was to avoid hiring my own advocate. He said that this would only prolong the case and cost the church more money. Instead, he instructed me as to how I should represent the church myself. He told me he would help me with what to say and also with how to prepare the legal documents required by the court. Next, he said that any time an appearance was required in court, I should come to him the night before, and he would help me prepare for what I would need to do the next day.

During these evening sessions, he played the role of the opposing lawyer, questioning me rigorously on the matters I was likely to face in the court. He was careful to tell me how I should answer in order to make the church's case stronger, and he also cautioned me on areas to avoid. I suppose he was putting me through a kind of law school, for the very limited purposes of representing the church in the matter of the disputed building.

He actually assured me that the judge was likely to look favorably on our situation, especially if, as he suspected, the opposing lawyers tried to cut corners. For the two years that the case dragged on, I followed his advice as closely as I could, and ultimately, the church received back the full use of the building. It was a very great victory that we could not have achieved without the behind-the-scenes help of our attorney friend.

One of the principal problems for non-Muslims living in a country governed by Islamic law is that taking the property of a non-Muslim is not considered a sin if it is related to *jihad*, or the struggle on behalf of Islam against unbelievers. For that reason, Said Ahmand was confident that he would prevail in court, and for that same reason, he saw no reason to meet with us in order to hear the church's reasonable understandings and requests. In most instances, his confidence would have been justified by the results. Only because of the quiet intercession of our attorney friend were we successful in our efforts.

In fact, as I look back on it, I can only conclude that God was protecting our work in Port Sudan, because there were many other situations in which we were able to advance the work of the church, even in the face of official and unofficial opposition.

After we had established a church in Kassala, for example, we purchased a piece of property from an individual on which we built a small church and Christian center. However, the local government officials ordered us to demolish the newly constructed building, because we had not obtained the necessary permits to build it. It is true that the laws of the country at that time—especially in the north—mandated that non-Islamic places of worship were required to be registered in advance and were subject to a number of licenses and regulations. This, of course, is only one way that the Muslim government sought and still seeks to control the spread of faiths other than Islam.

But we refused to tear down our building, and before we knew it, a bulldozer came and knocked down in a few minutes what it had taken us countless hours and many hard-won resources to build. We were stricken with sadness at this great loss.

However, the Christian center in Kassala was also serving many soldiers in the Sudanese Army who were Christians. Many of these men were from southern Sudan; they had been moved north and east in order to separate them from elements of the Sudanese People's Liberation Army who might otherwise have tried to recruit them. Still, when they found out about the bulldozing of the church, they complained to their officers. Before long, word reached the ear of Col. Deng Tem, who in turn took his protest to the principal commanders of the army.

In the meantime, I organized a protest march of the women and children in the church. About 2,000 of us walked in procession to the office of the provincial governor to make known our displeasure with the destruction of our church.

Between these efforts and the insistence of Colonel Tem, the pressure became sufficiently great that the governor decided to call a meeting. He told me that the government would rebuild the church and would make sure that it was properly registered in the name of the Episcopal Church of Sudan. I told him that I was very pleased with this decision. He then asked that I instruct the women and children to return to their homes and schools, and he also asked me to speak to the disaffected soldiers.

I was only too glad to do this. I urged the Christian community in Kassala to calm down and give the governor time to implement his plan of action. Before long, the church was rebuilt, the activities of the Christian center resumed in Kassala, and the Christian community rejoiced in the great deliverance of God.

During my years of service in Port Sudan, the church faced many similar difficulties. In fact, the agreement of the governor to rebuild and officially register the church in Kassala was the only time the Christian faith achieved such recognition by anyone associated with the Khartoum government.

❖ ❖ ❖

And then, in 1983, we, along with the rest of the country, witnessed the onset of a whole new round of repression, instigated by the Khartoum government's enactment of the infamous "September Laws," an initiative intended to impose Sharia law on the entire country, north and south, in violation of the principles of autonomy for the south that were part of the Addis Ababa Accords of 1972. With the ascendancy of Hassan al-Turabi, an Islamist lawyer, politician, and cleric, the central government renewed its determination to make all of Sudan a Muslim country—by force, if necessary.

Indeed, al-Turabi, who was attorney general of Sudan 1979–82, during the Nimeiry presidency, was the principal influence who led to Sudan serving as the host country and base of operations for Osama bin Laden during the period 1991–96, which is the same time during which the first attempt was made to destroy the New York World Trade Center and also when the attack was made on Khobar Towers in Saudi Arabia, a housing complex for US military personnel.

The September Laws, on top of the abuses of the Khartoum government that had been continuous and worsening virtually since the moment of the signing of the Addis Ababa Accords of 1972, created a situation that was ripe for an uprising, not only in the non-Muslim south, but also in places like Darfur and Nubia which, even though largely Muslim, were nevertheless either ignored or cynically exploited by the central government in Khartoum. And that is precisely what happened. The precipitating event actually occurred in the spring prior to the September Laws, when President Nimeiry ordered troops stationed in the south to redeploy in the north. This was in direct violation of the Addis Ababa Accords, which had guaranteed that members of the army who were from the south or were formerly Anya Nya soldiers would be allowed to stay near their homes. One of the units in Bor refused to obey the order, which led to the firing of the first shots of the Second Sudanese Civil War on May 16, 1983.

A leader soon emerged who was able to forge the various factions of disaffected Sudanese into a viable resistance force. This was John Garang, a man born in Twic East County, just as I was. He was educated in Tanzania then later in the United States and even received military training from the US Army, due to his former position of leadership in the Sudanese army. With the formation of the Sudanese People's Liberation Movement (SPLM) and its military wing, the Sudanese People's Liberation Army (SPLA), John Garang was able to effectively mobilize most of southern Sudan.[1]

Needless to say, in such an atmosphere of increasing hostility, my work with the church in Port Sudan became more and more difficult. Indeed, life for non-Muslims became difficult throughout the country. I have already related the events surrounding our worship center in Kassala, which, after much tension and strong opposition on the part of the Christians, came to a good conclusion. However, in the hostile atmosphere of the rising conflict, innocent people from the south were often arrested by the government in Khartoum, simply because they were suspected of being associated with the SPLM cause. I advocated on behalf of these southerners, spending much of my time and energy to make sure that they were not only protected from harm while they were imprisoned, but also to get them released as soon as possible.

For a time, the SPLA was in control of Kassala, which is some 300 miles south of Port Sudan, near the Eritrean border—and Amiskura, about

125 miles from Port Sudan. So, even though we were in the north of the country, there was still active fighting in the area, and part of the mission of the church was to provide safety for our people as best we could.

For its part, the Khartoum government employed the time-honored tactics that had served the Arab north so well for so many years. Agents provocateurs, working on behalf of northern interests, did all they could to exacerbate inter-tribal tensions in the south. Thus, longstanding rivalries between Nuer and Jieng, between Shilluk and Murle, and so forth, too often proved fertile ground for exploitation by those who wished the south to remain divided and weak.

War, both that visited by the north upon the south and that which arose from tribal rivalries in the south, led to widespread devastation. Whole villages were destroyed; southern Sudanese refugees—many of them young boys whose families had been slaughtered, abducted, or otherwise displaced—fled to Kenya, Uganda, and Ethiopia. Some 20,000 of these "lost boys," many of them from the Nilotic tribes of southern Sudan, traveled thousands of miles on foot through a war-torn country, seeking safety, food, and shelter. Hundreds died along the way, from disease, starvation, animal attack, and the violence of war.

But time and again, even amid such devastation, God provided for his people, and the church in Port Sudan not only survived, but prospered. During this same time, we built schools in Meim Parish and in High Phillip Gabush, along with the churches we established in and around Port Sudan. In fact, because of the large population of Christian men in the army who were stationed in and near Port Sudan, we established many churches in the eastern part of the country. Finally, in 1988, Port Sudan became a diocese, and I was appointed the first suffragan bishop of Port Sudan, a post that I held for seven years.

1. Natsios, *Sudan, South Sudan, and Darfur*, 93.

CHAPTER 7

Leadership Crisis, 1986–1992

Archbishop Elinana Ngalamu was enthroned October 11, 1976, as the first archbishop of the Episcopal Church of Sudan, when Sudan first became an independent province. Archbishop Elinana had been a vigorous and stalwart worker for the church for many years prior to this, having been a Christian since his baptism at age sixteen, in 1934.

He was a powerful preacher and teacher in his homeland in Western Equatoria State, in the south of the country, even daring to speak out against the forced Islamization of the south that was being carried out in the early 1960s, as the First Sudanese Civil War was intensifying. Because of his bold preaching, he was arrested by the government and sentenced to six months in prison for "disturbing the peace." After his release from prison, he was appointed archdeacon for the Moru-Dinka territory .

Narrowly escaping death at the hands of government forces, Elinana and many of the staff of Bishop Gwynne College, still in Mundri at that time, fled to Uganda, where he served among the southern Sudanese expatriates and in the territories controlled by Anya-Nya.[1] After the signing of the Addis Ababa Accords in 1972, he returned to Sudan and, with three others, became assistant to Bishop Oliver C. Allison, at that time Bishop of the Diocese of Sudan. The others appointed as assistant bishops with Elinana were Jeremiah Kufuta Dotira, Assistant Bishop of Yambio; Butrus Tea, Assistant Bishop of Khartoum; and Benjamin Wani Yugusuk, assistant bishop of Rumbek. Upon Allison's retirement, Elinana became his successor as Bishop of the Diocese of Sudan. Then, two years later, when Sudan became an independent province, he was enthroned as archbishop and primate by the Archbishop of Canterbury at that time, the Most Reverend Donald Coggan.

Under Archbishop Elinana's leadership, the Episcopal Church of Sudan made many important advances, both nationally and internationally. He established assistance programs for the many refugees coming from Uganda and Zaire (now the Democratic Republic of the Congo) in those years, and he also established housing projects and vocational training institutes. Even more importantly, he played a pivotal role in the establishment of the Sudan Council of Churches in 1960. He also wrote hymns in the Moru language and made other contributions to the development of indigenous worship. He built bridges of trust between various Christian fellowships throughout Sudan and also forged strong relationships with the Anglican Church in the United Kingdom and with the Episcopal Church in the United States. He was a truly great and visionary leader, and he accomplished all this during some of the most difficult and bloody times in the history of Sudan.[2]

❖ ❖ ❖

In 1986, Archbishop Elinana made a visit to the United States, partly to strengthen ties between the Episcopal Church there and the Episcopal Church of Sudan. Prior to his departure, however, he had questioned the provincial secretary, the office by then occupied by Reverend Canon Kanyikwa, regarding some properties Kanyikwa had acquired. Apparently, Archbishop Elinana was uncertain that the properties had been obtained properly. This was not resolved before the archbishop left on his trip to the US, however. He temporarily suspended Reverend Canon Kanyikwa and appointed a committee to investigate the matter. The group was chaired by Bishop Benjamin Yugusuk of Rumbek, whom Archbishop Elinana had appointed as Acting Archbishop while he was traveling.

According to the constitution of the Episcopal Church of Sudan, Rev. Michael Lugari became Acting Provincial Secretary during the suspension of Reverend Canon Kanyikwa. In later years, Lugari would be appointed Bishop of Rejof Diocese. He served the church faithfully until his retirement in 2010. In 2016, Bishop Lugari went to his eternal rest, leaving behind him a legacy of service to God's people.

Having made these dispositions of the various duties and responsibilities of the Episcopal Church of Sudan, Archbishop Elinana had traveled to the United States, as was his right as primate of an independent province of the Episcopal Church. However, he did not inform a certain key person of his intention to go there, and this would lead to problems.

Bishop Oliver Allison was the Diocesan Bishop of Sudan, prior to Sudan becoming an independent province with its own archbishop. He had been deeply involved in the work of the Church in Sudan since coming there in 1938 under an appointment by the Missionary Society of the Anglican Church. In 1974, two years before the elevation of Archbishop Elinana, Bishop Allison retired from active ministry but remained very deeply connected to the work in Sudan as a member of the Sudan Church Association, based in London. For some reason, Bishop Allison did not think it proper for Archbishop Elinana to travel to the United States without informing him. He was quite displeased, in fact.

Bishop Allison was sufficiently provoked by Archbishop Elinana's actions that he wrote a secret letter to Bishop Lugari concerning Archbishop Elinana. The letter requested that Lugari, in his capacity as Acting Provincial Secretary, call a provincial synod for the purpose of considering the replacement of Archbishop Elinana.

As these developments were unfolding, Archbishop Elinana, who had just returned from the US, fell very ill in Khartoum. Significantly, Acting Archbishop Yugusuk did not come to Khartoum to welcome Archbishop Elinana upon his return. It is possible that Bishop Benjamin was unable to come due to financial problems or because of difficulties posed by the war. It is also possible that the active rumor of Bishop Allison's letter to Michael Lugari played some part in his decision. But for whatever reason or combination of reasons, he did not come.

Those of us around Archbishop Elinana were trying desperately to find a way to convey him to Nairobi, where he could receive the treatment he needed. Of course, with an active war going on in the country, this was very difficult. And while we were in the midst of these efforts, we all received a letter from Reverend Canon Kanyikwa, who was still officially under investigation, informing us of an emergency synod of bishops to be held in Juba. Further, the letter listed the names of the delegates who were to attend.

None of this was in accordance with the constitution of the Episcopal Church of Sudan. First of all, a synod should not be called unless the sitting archbishop can be in attendance, which clearly Archbishop Elinana was too ill to do. Next, each diocese in the province is tasked with selecting its own delegates to attend the synod; delegates are not unilaterally appointed by the provincial officers. Indeed, few of the Jieng dioceses were consulted at all about sending delegates. Instead, it became clear that the delegates had been hand-picked by someone who presumably wished to see that the synod had a certain outcome.

Those of us in Khartoum sent Bishop Benjamin Mangaar, of Yirol Diocese, to Juba to urge Bishop Yugusuk and Reverend Canon Kanyikwa to delay the synod until Archbishop Elinana had recovered enough to attend. However, this message was summarily rejected, whereupon Bishop Mangaar distanced himself from the proceedings. Against the counsel of his fellow bishops, Acting Archbishop Yugusuk went ahead with organizing the emergency synod.

I believe to this day that Bishop Yugusuk was acting in good faith, based on the information he was receiving. However, I also believe that those around him were not providing him with all the facts that should inform such a drastic course of action. And indeed, this controversial emergency synod, organized specifically to insure the ouster of Archbishop Elinana, would have bitterly divisive consequences for the Episcopal Church of Sudan for several years to come.

So, for a time there were, in effect, two archbishops in Sudan: Archbishop Elinana, who had the support of those of us in and around Khartoum; and Benjamin Yugusuk, who was supported by all of the bishops in the south of the country, with the exceptions of Bishop Eluzai Munda and Bishop Nathaniel Garang, who were essentially isolated from the rest of us by the ongoing civil war.

Yugusuk and his supporters also enjoyed the backing of Bishop Allison, who at this time was associated with the Diocese of Salisbury, in England. Significant financial assets from these sources came to bear on the schism, which provided a great advantage for Bishop Yugusuk and his partisans.

Nevertheless, those of us who stood by Archbishop Elinana remained determined that everything should be done according to the church constitution. We made appeals among our churches in the north for money, and we formed a committee of high-level church leaders to advise Archbishop Elinana and to consider the various courses of action available to us.

One of those actions was to confer with the chancellor for the province, His Excellency John Wall Makech, who would represent us in any legal actions that might arise from the controversy. Following South Sudanese independence in 2011, Makech became president of the Supreme Court of South Sudan. Later, Isaac Kanisa would assume these duties for us in Juba. Meanwhile, the other faction had appointed James Lomala as their chancellor. This proved to be an unfortunate choice for them, because subsequently, when the matter did go to the court, we were able to successfully challenge Lomala's qualifications, since he was not a duly appointed lawyer. This resulted in Lomala being dismissed from the courtroom by the judge, which was a serious blow to those who supported Benjamin Yugusuk. So, even though the other party had greater financial resources, we felt that we had the allegiance of a greater number of the Christians in the country, as well as superior representation in the court. And, of course, we strongly believed that we were rightly upholding the church constitution.

Despite all this, Benjamin Yugusuk, acting as archbishop, confirmed as bishops of various dioceses Butrus Kwo, Michael Lugari, Balus Idris, and Gabriel Roric. At the same time, Archbishop Elinana confirmed Kedhekia B. Mabior, Levi Hassen, Benjamin John Rwate, Matiya Renga, Peter El-Biresh, Benjamin Mangaar, Ruben Maciir, Ephriam Natana, Wilson Arop, and me. Archbishop Elinana took this extraordinary action because of necessity in the face of the growing opposition to his primacy and to counter the actions being taken by Yugusuk and his faction.

And so, for a time, all the dioceses were operating in this rather fractured fashion, both in and around Khartoum, in the north, and similarly in and around Juba, in the south. It was a very confusing and distressing state of affairs.

❖ ❖ ❖

In the spirit of the eighteenth chapter of St. Matthew, where Jesus instructs his disciples about how they should go and talk to a brother or sister who has done some wrong against them, a group of us began meeting together quietly, trying to develop some way to resolve the division in the Church, which was greatly hampering our ministry impact during a time of intensifying war between the Sudanese People's Liberation Army (SPLA) and the forces of the Islamist government in Khartoum. Our suffering nation desperately needed the healing that only the Church can provide, and yet we were divided over this question of leadership and succession. It was a tragedy, and a few of us were determined to seek a solution. To his great credit, Bishop Michael Lugari, from the Yugusuk group, was faithful in his efforts with Bishop Levi Hassan of Ibba and I as we tried to forge a compromise that would allow the church to move forward in a unified way. For some six years we met together; at the same time we were ministering to our various dioceses and dealing with the dangers and complications posed by the ongoing civil war.

In 1992, as we were coming closer to a solution for the problem, Bishop Elinana, whose health had been deteriorating all during this time, went to be with the Lord. With the passing of this faithful servant, unity came to the Episcopal Church of Sudan. Leaders and others from both sides of the former conflict came together at the Cathedral of All Saints in Khartoum on November 8, 1992, as we laid to rest Archbishop Elinana's earthly remains. The next day, a gathering of bishops from all of Sudan confirmed the leadership of Benjamin Yugusuk as the second Archbishop of Sudan. Years later, as archbishop, I would have Elinana Ngalamu's remains disinterred and brought to Juba for re-burial, at the heart of Christian South Sudan.

Not long after this, in 1995, Archbishop Yugusuk would confirm me as Bishop of the newly created Renk Diocese, in the far north of Upper Nile State. With this appointment, a new and important phase of ministry began.

1. Anglican Communion News Service, "Article from the Episcopal Church of Sudan," November 10, 2008 [online]. Available at http://www.anglican-news.org/news/2008/11/article-from-the-episcopal-church-of-sudan.aspx (accessed September 25, 2016).
2. Dictionary of African Christian Biography, "Elinana Ja'bi Ngalamu Dudu, 1918 to 1992" [online]. Available at http://www.dacb.org/stories/sudan/ngalamu_elinana.html (accessed September 24, 2016).

CHAPTER 8

Renk Diocese, 1995–2007

Renk, at the northern end of Upper Nile State, is almost two hundred miles upriver from Malakal, the provincial capital. However, it has been an important center for preaching and evangelism in the church for many years. Renk gained greater importance in 1967, when a number of government officials were relocated there from Malakal. Many of these people were members of the Episcopal Church of Sudan, but historically, Renk and its surrounding area have been known as a majority Muslim place, largely because of its proximity to the northern part of the country. Even the Jieng who live in the Renk area are mostly Muslim.

For a long time, Renk was part of the Bor Archdeaconry. Many priests came from both Bor and Malakal to Renk in order to help establish it as a strong outpost for the Church, during the period 1960–71. Many distinguished priests hail from Renk, including Rev. Francis Moriebe, Rev. Bullen Dole—who became Bishop of Lui—and Rev. David Alaak Kuot. Between 1972 and 1982, Rev. Kedhekia B. Mabior, while he was Archdeacon of Bor, made many visits to Renk. Mabior would one day be appointed Bishop of Malakal Diocese.

❖ ❖ ❖

I began visiting Renk in 1984 and continued working there for four years, working with the Christians in the town of Renk to build a church. I also made a number of evangelistic trips there and also to points farther north, including Kinana, Assalaaya, and the region of Gezira, near Khartoum. By 1986, I was the pastor of Port Sudan Parish and in 1988, I was asked to become caretaker bishop of Kongor Diocese, in Twic East County, Jonglei State. These two areas were very far apart, and exercising my pastoral duties was challenging, to say the least.

In 1989 I sent Rev. Jacob Ajak Deng (now deceased) to become pastor in Renk, and this was about the same time that Renk was organized as an independent diocese, rather than an archdeaconry in the oversight of Bor or Malakal. Reverend Jacob was a crucial partner in building the diocese.

❖ ❖ ❖

During this time, the war between the SPLA and the Khartoum government was still in full force, and any Christian activity in a predominantly Muslim area was almost always viewed with official suspicion. Because of this, the government security forces arrested me on one of my early visits to Renk. They warned me that I should return to Khartoum and discontinue my activities in Renk. Naturally, I did not take their advice, and soon after, I was arrested again, this time along with my companion, Rev. John Bul Atem. After being released with a second warning from the security forces, I called a meeting of various church leaders in the town, from all other Christian denominations.

To our surprise, we learned that all the Christian leaders were being called in by the security forces, usually by 6:00 a.m. Typically they would not be released until 7:00 p.m.

Upon learning this, I instructed the other priests to stop going to the security forces' compound. I told them that if they were questioned, they should tell the officers that the bishop had instructed them not to go, and that the officers should come and talk to me.

Sure enough, when the priests stopped answering the summons of the security forces, the police went to find out what had happened. When they received their answer, they sent a fleet of cars and motorcycles to the church, with sirens blaring. They announced their intention to take me into custody, but I refused to go with them. This was on Saturday, and when the standoff continued until Sunday and the Christians of Renk were not able to attend prayers as usual, there was a great uproar in the Christian community. It was the beginning of a revival in Renk.

❖❖❖

After unity was achieved under Archbishop Yugusuk, I went to Renk as bishop of a relatively new diocese, with its headquarters in Renk Town. It was officially known as the Diocese of Northern Upper Nile. At this time, the only clergy in the diocese were Rev. Jacob Ajok Deng (now deceased) and I. There was much work to be done!

Meanwhile my wife and I had received the distressing news, in 1991, that my wife's parents had been killed when a rival faction of the SPLA, led by a man named Dr. Riak Machar, had overrun Twic East County. This was a very sad time for us, and yet, because of the violence that was still prevalent in most of the country, there was nothing we could do.

Indeed, because of the ongoing war and the official repression of all religions other than Islam, we had to be constantly on guard against government intrusion and even threats. In 1995, for example, a government commission in Renk ordered a Catholic school, founded by the Comboni Missionaries, closed down in order to convert it into a training facility for military activities.

I called a meeting of all the church leaders in the area and asked them to mobilize their congregations to protest this unlawful act by the government. Very soon a large number of Christians of various denominations had gathered at the school, and some women even managed to get inside the school compound. They began singing Christian songs, along with a few SPLA-inspired liberation songs.

The military officers in the school compound contacted the local military commander and told him that the SPLA was in the compound—what should they do? The commander responded by sending a small detachment of soldiers in a car. Some of the soldiers were southerners, however, and when they arrived and heard the people singing, they joined in. Soon, they reported back to the commander that there were no SPLA soldiers in the compound; it was just ordinary citizens who were protesting the seizure of the church school.

H. E. Said Tara Morji, the commander, went to the government commission that had ordered the seizure of the school and recommended, first, the removal of military personnel from the school compound; this was done. Next, a meeting was scheduled among Morji, the commissioner of Renk, and local church leaders. In that meeting, we demanded that the school be returned and that the school's headmaster and two watchmen, who had been previously taken into custody, be released.

The commissioner met our conditions, the school was returned to the Catholic Church—in whose control it remains to this day—and we had achieved a great victory because of our Christian unity in the face of government repression.

❖ ❖ ❖

But there was more to do in Renk than respond to crises. One of my first priorities upon my confirmation as bishop was to put in place a five-year strategic plan for helping the church grow and mature in the faith. And evangelism was at the top of my list.

I invited a number of priests to come and join the work in Renk Diocese: Rev. John Bul Atem, Venerable (Ven.) Abraham Noon Jiel, Rev. Sapara Adeer Kuir, and Rev. Joseph Garang Atem, who eventually succeeded me as the bishop of Renk Diocese. A second team was composed of Evangelist Michael Miakol Lang and Evangelist Rueben Chol Yung. The third team was made up of Rev. Barnaba Madul Juac (now deceased), whom I posted in Wad-Akona Sub-Parish, west of the river. Rev. Sapana Mawut Bol and Evangelist Peter Chuol Mabut were posted in Geiger Sub-Parish, not far north of Renk and east of the Nile. The fourth team consisted of Rev. Paul Ajang Thiel and Peter Atem Jok.

Within five years, we were enjoying great success in evangelism. We opened church centers in Paloc, Thing-Rial, Marial, Panhomdit, Khoradaar, Jalhak, Lathbior, Wad Kona, Geiger, and Renk Town, in addition to a preaching center in Maban, near the border with Ethiopia.

Much of our evangelistic work was accomplished at great risk, just behind government lines during the civil war. As the northern government forces would make an advance, civilians would come under government control. Often, the government's first attempt would be to try to convert the people to Islam as a part of jihad. To work against these efforts, we would go into areas that had recently come under government control and preach Christianity. Though we were often exposed to danger by doing this, we believed we were under the protection of God while doing this important work.

During this time, two incidents occurred that I will never forget. On one occasion, I was traveling to a place called Melut, in Upper Nile State, in a lorry with a number of my fellow evangelists, both male and female.

Soldiers from the northern government halted our lorry and commanded us to get out. When we did, they began separating the men from the women. I had a very bad feeling about this, and I tried to intervene, but the soldiers pushed me aside.

I was very afraid that we were about to be brutalized and killed, but at about this time, one of the commanders of the battalion arrived at the scene, demanding to know what was happening. This man recognized one of the women evangelists, Rev. Grace Isaiah, who was from the commander's home state, Western Equatoria. They began speaking together in Azanda, one of the principal dialects of that region. When I saw this taking place, I felt great relief flooding through me.

Soon, the commander ordered the soldiers to release us and allow us to get back in our lorry. We went on our way, praising God. We knew that if the commander from Western Equatoria had not arrived and recognized Reverend Grace, the women would likely have been raped and the rest of us would have been gunned down as we tried to resist. Later, they would say we were rebel agents, and the matter would be completely forgotten by the government.

In the second incident, I was traveling with another evangelism team to Khor Adaar, in Melut County. Our transportation was by means of a trailer being pulled by a farm tractor, because this was a remote area, and the roads were very poor. Government troops were following us; our intention was to eventually go and baptize people around Khor Adaar.

As we traveled, we flew above our vehicle a white flag bearing a cross, to signify that we were religious workers and noncombatants. But perhaps because of the government troops traveling so near to us, we came under ambush by forces of the SPLA.

However, we were once again saved from danger when the SPLA fighters recognized our flag. Even though the government troops were near, the rebel fighters held their fire. The government troops went around us and continued on toward Khor Adaar. Later, when we arrived at their location, we attempted to offer the soliders our greetings. They wanted to know who we were and where we were going, and we answered that we were religious workers who were going to Khor Adaar for a celebration—this was happening during the Christmas season. They allowed us to go on our way without further problems.

❖ ❖ ❖

In 1990, I had enjoyed the opportunity to attend Haggai Institute in Singapore in order to obtain additional training in Christian leadership, and in that same year I attended the Senior Leadership Management Training offered by Christian Organizations Research and Advisory Trust for Africa (CORAT Africa), which took place in Kenya. So, in 1996, when I had the opportunity to travel to the United States for advanced education and training, I was delighted, knowing the importance of such an experience for my ability to continue to lead the church in Sudan.

I studied for a year at Virginia Seminary, in Alexandria, completing the course for a diploma in theology. Not only did I receive valuable ministry training, but I also was able to forge many wonderful relationships with Episcopal churches and leaders in Virginia and Chicago. These partnerships would produce many great benefits for our work with the Christians in Renk Diocese and throughout Sudan. During my time of study at Virginia Seminary I had the chance to meet Rev. Geoffrey Hor, the parish priest of St. Paul's Church in Alexandria. I also became acquainted with Andrew Maro, the parish priest of St. Mary's Church in Arlington, Virginia. Other persons I met during this time included Professor Allen Davis of Duke Divinity School, Rev. Clement of Christ Church Parish and Russ Randel, one of his parishioners, and Bishop Francis Gray, the assistant bishop of the Diocese of Virginia. Bishop Gray contributed generously to the eventual construction of St. Matthew Cathedral in Renk Town; he personally raised some 50 percent of the cost of construction.

As a result of the good relationships I developed while in Virginia, I was able to preach at a conference and bring to the attention of many American Christians the problems faced by the Christians in southern Sudan. At that same conference I also was privileged to meet Jacqueline "Jackie" Crous, who has been a faithful partner in our efforts for many years since.

My travel to the US indeed provided the first connection for Renk Diocese with the outside world. Building on the friendships I established at St. Paul Episcopal Church and Christ Church in Alexandria, Virginia; Church of the Apostles in Fairfax, Virginia; St. Michael Episcopal Church in Chicago, and other wonderful churches in the United States, we were able to form important covenants that reached across the ocean, the deserts, and the jungles to unite believers on opposite sides of the world in the common cause of God's kingdom.

In each case when I had the opportunity to form such a covenant with sister congregations in the US, I asked them for three things: that we might be in constant prayer for one another; that our brothers and sisters in the US might offer help to Sudanese refugees in the United States; and that, out of their generosity, they might aid us in our efforts to comfort and help those displaced by the war in Sudan.

It still delights my soul to recall the many ways this covenant has borne fruit. In 1998, a seven-member delegation from the US churches came to Renk Diocese to see first-hand the work we were doing. Upon their return, they wrote a report that resulted in widespread support among

US churches for our work in Sudan, including vital financial support that helped us build schools, health clinics, and worship centers, and also to provide training and support for our faithful church servants.

❖❖❖

The first diocesan council for Renk Diocese had been formed in April 1992. The bishop prior to my appointment, Rt. Rev. Benjamin Wanni Yugusuk, appointed the council to help with the preparations for Renk's promotion to an independent diocese. I chaired the council, and I enjoyed the invaluable assistance of Thiong Akuei as Diocesan Secretary, Rev. Jacob Ajak, Bior Kuer Aguer, Joseph Mading Ajing, Daniel Atem, Awal Deng A, Samuel Lueth Agot, Solomon Makuac Agot, Sultan Deng Any-ieth, and Lay Readers Grace Isaiah, James Aboy Amul, Gordon Mathews, and Goliver Barnaba. With the help of the council, we created the first five-year plan for the new diocese.

Then, in 1997, as bishop of the diocese, I directed the creation of the second five-year strategic plan, which included the continuation and completion of a number of programs that had been initiated as part of the first plan, begun in 1992. We made great strides in spiritual development of Christians in the diocese, in addition to much evangelistic outreach. We also built St. Matthew's Cathedral, additional churches, and other facilities, and provided desperately needed humanitarian assistance services to the many people displaced by the ongoing war. We could not have succeeded in these efforts without the gracious financial assistance of churches and individual Christians in the United States, many of whom I had met and formed friendships with during my year of study there.

As I reflect on the many good things we accomplished in Renk Diocese during those years, I cannot help but remember the faithful servants who contributed their time, talents, and energy to our ministry. Amos Awan de Gak, who served from 1994 to 1999 as our Diocesan Development Coordinator, held a bachelor's degree in agriculture and a postgraduate degree in management. His leadership was vital, as was that of

Duom Kuol Ageer. With a bachelor's degree in commerce and a postgraduate degree in development studies, Ageer served us as a financial advisor from 1996 to 2000. Lucy Small Mogga was our secretary and office manager from 1996 to 2000. She had completed her Sudanese School Certificate in Secreterial and Computer Knowledge. We were advised in legal matters by our diocesan chancellor, Majok Mading Majok, who served from 1996 to 2000 and held a bachelor's degree in law and a postgraduate diploma in foreign relations. His depth of experience with the office of the Sudan Attorney General was invaluable. In 2000, Majok became the chancellor of the province when Bishop Joseph Marona was elevated as archbishop and primate. Finally, Dora Agrey served as my office assistant and manager. Without these good people, I would have been unable to accomplish what was done in Renk Diocese.

❖❖❖

As part of the original five-year plan in 1992, the diocese had started a basic school, with financing assistance from the government of the Netherlands. We used this money to build two rooms, each five meters by five meters in area. From 1995 to 2000, Christian Aid, a United Kingdom organization, took over the financing of the school. We used grants from this agency to build additional classrooms and a sanitary latrine, to procure school furniture, books, dry rations for the children's meals, teacher transport allowances, and a grinding mill to process food.

In 1997 and 1998, the school was blessed by partnering with four parishes in the United States. These American Christians also provided aid for schools in the archdeaconry to the south of Renk, and we received funding from the Church of the Apostles in Fairfax, Virginia, in 1999, in order to establish a kindergarten in Geiger Parish. In that same year, we opened Renk Bible School, offering a course in theology from January to May; thirty students attended.

The agriculture program of the diocese was another central initiative by which we provided not only desperately needed food for the people of Renk and the surrounding area, but also offered training and work, along with achieving a degree of capability to sustain and provide for our own needs. In 1995, we received a $24,000 grant from the United Thanks Offering of the Women's Union of the Episcopal Church of the United States of America (ECUSA). We used this money to purchase a tractor, a trailer, and a water tank. Although the program got off to a rocky start in 1996 due to inexperience in management and limited finances, we received a generous gift of $10,000 the following year from St. Paul Episcopal Church of Alexandria, Virginia, which we used to purchase a seed drill. We were unable to cultivate any crops in 1997 or 1998 because there was no experienced agriculturalist whose services were available to us. But in the 1998–99 season we were able to place under cultivation an area of about 1,000 *feddans* (about 1,038 acres). This land produced some 3,000 bags of sorghum. We distributed about a third of this to church workers and used most of the rest to provide aid for displaced persons (about 100 bags were used to make in-kind payment for the rental of the land).

❖❖❖

The importance of our ability to produce at least part of our own food was highlighted by an incident that occurred in 2000, in connection with Chinese oil exploration in Upper Nile State. In the areas of Melut and Paloch, some ninety miles south of Renk Town, the Khartoum government or its agents put to the torch about eighty villages, because they wanted to clear the area in order to make things easier for the Chinese to conduct their oil exploration and drilling and also to assert the government's claim on the valuable resources to be extracted.[1] All the people in these villages were instantly made homeless and destitute by this cruel action, and it was up to the Church to help.

I gathered about seventy bags of sorghum and traveled south, toward the area where the destruction had occurred. But when I reached Jalah, about halfway between Renk Town and Paloch, I was halted by government troops. For six hours I argued and negotiated with them, trying to convince them that I was not taking the food to the SPLA, but rather to the starving people from the eighty burned villages. Despite these efforts, many innocent people died needlessly because of this incident.

Such a terrible circumstance also points to the importance of another initiative we established for the diocese: the health program. Beginning with the first five-year plan in 1992, we identified the importance of providing health care and aid for the many children displaced by the war and also for our church workers. In 1999, Renk Diocese applied to take over the duty of running a health clinic that had been previously overseen by the Sudan Council of Churches' (SCC) Primary Healthcare Programme (PHCP). Our application was the culmination of aspects of the SCC program, combined with our intention to develop our own effort, which subsequently became known as Episcopal Church of Sudan Clinic/Renk Diocese.

The Diocese of Virginia and other friendly partners in the US graciously underwrote this important initiative. The Diocese of Virginia alone contributed $20,000 toward this important effort, funds that were primarily used to pay medical personnel and to purchase drugs for the clinic. Once again, my contacts in the United States had paid great dividends for the work of the Church in Sudan.

❖ ❖ ❖

Perhaps the crowning achievement of my ministry in Renk Diocese occurred in 2006, when we were able, by the grace of God and with the help of many generous Christians in Sudan and the United States, to finish building St. Matthew's Cathedral in Renk Town. That we were able to do this, in a town so near to the north of the country and during a time of ongoing hostility between the Khartoum government and the SPLA, is one of the great miracles I have witnessed in my life.

It is important to understand that the true glory of St. Matthew Cathedral is not as a monument to me or even to the people who labored with their hands and hearts to build it. Its significance lies in the fact of where it stands: on the border between north and south, between Muslim and

Christian. In building this cathedral, the Christians of Renk have said to the world, "We are here, and we mean to stay here." The Cathedral of St. Matthew in Renk Town is, by its very existence, a public proclamation of our faith and our confidence in God. Despite war, despite repression, despite governmental and social pressure, the Christians of Renk have raised this house of worship as a testament to belief.

Many Christians in Renk Diocese have made great personal sacrifices to assure the building of the cathedral. They have persisted despite often being hungry, poor, and unemployed. They gave freely of their time and the labor of their hands. As St. Paul said of the Christians in Macedonia, they first of all gave themselves, and then they gave of their resources. They gave because they believed in the vision and in the importance of establishing this house of worship and ministry.

It was one of the proudest moments of my life when, on February 28, 2006, the Most Reverend Rowan Williams, Archbishop of Canterbury, consecrated St. Matthew Cathedral in Renk Town. Many of our friends from the United States attended the event, as well as the archbishop of the Episcopal Church of Sudan and many other dignitaries and church leaders. It was a day I will never forget.

❖ ❖ ❖

In 2007, His Grace Archbishop Joseph Marona, who had succeeded Archbishop Yugusuk in 2000, asked me to become caretaker bishop of the Diocese of Yei, which is far in the south, very near the borders with the Democratic Republic of the Congo and Uganda. This was quite distant from Renk Diocese, but it was necessary for me to undertake this duty temporarily, since the bishop of the diocese, Rt. Rev. Henry Luta Adeba, was on sabbatical leave for study in the United Kingdom.

When I arrived for my first visit to Yei Diocese, I learned that some of the Christians there were not happy that a Jieng had been appointed as their spiritual leader. Most of the people of Yei Diocese are of the Kakwa tribe, and having a Jieng bishop was not sitting well with them.

As I met with a number of my parishioners in Yei, they asked me to go back where came from, because "Jieng bishops are not wanted in this place." I asked them if they were primarily Kakwa, or primarily Christian. When they did not answer me, I told them that I had come to Yei to help and minister to the Christians, whether they were Kakwa or something else. After that, we did not have too much trouble with people grumbling about tribes. In fact, while I served as caretaker bishop in Yei, I was able to confirm about 5,000 new Christians.

❖ ❖ ❖

During my ministry in Renk Diocese, we accomplished many more things than those I have mentioned above. We established an active vocational training and spiritual formation program for women in the diocese; we set up a river transport system for the church and purchased the *Papyrus*, a boat that the church utilized actively, especially for evangelism; we provided postgraduate training for church personnel; we established three archdeaconries for the diocese that became self-sustaining organizations by 2000; and we called together a distinguished committee of church leaders and highly qualified laypersons—some with international credentials—to draft the first constitution for the Diocese of Renk, which we presented successfully to the diocesan synod in 1999.

In all these matters, of course, it was my joy to serve. In fact, ever since first being appointed as an evangelist for the Christian community in Khartoum, all the way back in 1971, it seemed to me that God had led me from one place of blessing to another. By doing my best to follow his call, I was the one who was receiving great joy, even in times of trouble and danger.

But very soon, God would call me to an even greater purpose, and an even larger field of service. And the path to that call would begin with a surprising announcement.

1. See, for example, Jemera Rone, *Sudan, Oil, and Human Rights* (New York: Human Rights Watch, 2003), 317.

CHAPTER 9

Fourth Archbishop of Sudan

Joseph Marona became archbishop of Sudan in 2000, succeeding Benjamin Yugusuk, who had served as primate of the church in Sudan for ten years. Originally from Maridi, in Western Equatoria State and very near the border with the Democratic Republic of Congo, Marona began attending classes at an elementary school run by the Church Missionary Society in 1954, when he was eleven years old. He was able to obtain his certification to teach in 1958 and taught Arabic in Tali and Lui until the First Sudanese Civil War forced him into exile in Uganda.

Following his return, he became interested in ministry and, like me, went to Bishop Gwynne College in Mundri for theological studies. After being ordained a deacon, he was appointed a priest and subsequently consecrated as bishop of the newly created Diocese of Maridi. For many years he was active in translating the Bible into his native language of Baka and also with teaching.

He was elevated to archbishop, with the expectation that he would serve a ten-year term, as Archbishop Yugusuk had done before him. But we were all surprised when, in December 2007, after completing the eighth year of his primacy, he announced his retirement, due to deteriorating health.

The church called an emergency general synod, and three names were placed forward by the gathered bishops: Rt. Rev. Ezekiel Kondo, Bishop of the Diocese of Khartoum; Rt. Rev. Francis Loyo, Bishop of the Diocese of Rokon; and I. Subsequently, I was elected to become the fourth archbishop and primate of the Episcopal Church of Sudan.

The country was in a somewhat different and more favorable place by this time. In 2005, after more than two decades of fighting, the Sudanese People's Liberation Movement, or SPLM (with the Sudanese People's Liberation Army, SPLA, as its military wing) signed the Comprehensive Peace Agreement (CPA) with the Khartoum government, bringing to an end— on an official basis, at least—the military conflict between the northern and southern parts of the country. The CPA afforded autonomy to the south, establishing the Government of South Sudan, with its administrative capital at Juba. The agreement also guaranteed a southern referendum on independence from the north by 2011, and it removed the south of the country from the jurisdiction of sharia law and from compulsory instruction in Arabic.

After the signing of the CPA, it was much easier to travel and to do many other things. For example, I was able, in 2005, to return to Twic East County and to complete payment of the dowry for my wife to Makuei Aguer, her uncle, who had assumed management of the affairs of my deceased father-in-law. Increased ease of travel also meant that many refugees returned to the south from other countries and even places in northern Sudan where they had fled. Also, many among the southern Sudanese diaspora—people who were living in the United States, Europe, and other places—came back to the country. The government of southern Sudan was mostly Christian, which certainly made things a bit easier. However, much of the land belonging to the Episcopal Church of Sudan that was taken in the 1960s was still not returned, because it had been distributed to private individuals during the period of conflict.

❖ ❖ ❖

My election as archbishop occurred on the Feast of St. Valentine, 2008. As soon as my election was confirmed, the synod set the date for my enthronement at All Saints Cathedral in Juba; it would take place on April 20, 2008. Over the next two months, there was much to be done.

Some twenty bishops, from the various dioceses in both the north and south of the country, would be coming to Juba, with their families, and would need accommodations. Many leaders of the church from all over the world would also be attending, and we would need to assist with these arrangements, as well. Rt. Rev. Peter Amidi, Bishop of the Diocese of Lanya, chaired the Enthronement Committee, and he soon informed us that the principal celebrant of the ceremony would be the Most Rev. Emmanuel Kolini, Archbishop of the Anglican Province of Rwanda. Archbishop Kolini was also chair of the Council of Anglican Primates of Africa (CAPA). Additionally, eleven bishops and thirty-one lay leaders from other countries were expected to arrive in Juba to celebrate this event with us. Martin Barahona, primate of the church in Central America; Mauricio Andrade, Archbishop of the Province of Brazil; Miguel Tamayo, Bishop of Uruguay and interim bishop of Cuba; Jonathan Hart, Bishop of Liberia; Bishop James Ochiel of the Diocese of Southern Nyanza in Kenya; and Bishop Coadjutor Shannon Johnston of the Diocese of Virginia were just a few of the church leaders from abroad who graced us with their presence. Additionally, Bishop David James from the Diocese of Bradford, England, attended as an emissary of the Most Rev. Rowan Williams, Archbishop of Canterbury. From the Diocese of Salisbury, the two suffragan bishops, Rt. Rev. Stephen Conway and Rt. Rev. Tim Thornton, traveled to Juba for the ceremony.

Among the government leaders in attendance was the president of the new Government of South Sudan and First Vice President of the Republic of Sudan, Salva Kiir Mayardit. Alexander Baumgarten, international policy analyst in the Office of Government Relations for the Episcopal Church; Janette O'Neill, director of African Operations for the Episcopal Relief and Development agency; Rev. Emmanuel Sserwadda, officer for Africa Partnerships for the Episcopal Church; Richard Parkins, former director of Episcopal Migration Ministries; and Kimberly Stietz, director for international policy in the Washington, DC, office of the Evangelical Lutheran Church in America came to Juba for the glad occasion. I was especially gratified to see Rev. J. Barney Hawkins, executive director of the Center for Anglican Communion Studies at Virginia Theological Seminary, where I studied in 1996.

I have often reflected on the interesting coincidence that the very first Anglican priest for the church in Sudan, Rt. Rev. Daniel Deng Atong, who was consecrated in 1955 in Uganda, was Jieng. And now, with my enthronement, a Jieng was the fourth archbishop of Sudan. But this is not primarily about bringing notoriety to myself or even my clan; it is a sign of how far the church had advanced in my country, even during fifty years of almost-constant conflict. It is a testament to the faithfulness of God to preserve his people.

On the day of the ceremony, a marching band and choir led the procession to the cathedral. Large crowds of people from Juba and elsewhere gathered all along the route to cheer, and hundreds of them stood outside the cathedral to watch the enthronement proceedings on large television screens that were set up to accommodate the throngs who could not come inside the packed cathedral. The service and the speeches outside the cathedral that followed were punctuated by cheering, singing in English and Arabic, by Jieng calls, by applause, and by many other spontaneous expressions of joy.

To all of us gathered there, it felt like a new day for southern Sudan and for the Episcopal Church of Sudan. We heard messages of encouragement and hope, and as a result, we felt filled with hope ourselves. And in our country at that time, following a war that had lasted more than twenty years and had claimed more than two million lives, with millions more displaced from their homes, hope was the most indispensable thing.

Archbishop Kolini, in his homily, reminded us all that "Rome was not built in a day," urging us to have patience as together we built a new Juba and a new South Sudan. He assured us that "God has a plan," and that we had to be strong in order to "be a good bridge between the north and the south."

In my remarks, I told all those assembled that as a church, we were there to stay. "We are not going anywhere," I said to them. "We want a united Episcopal Church."[1]

❖ ❖ ❖

Indeed, as I assumed the primacy that day, the subject of unity was very much on my mind and heart. I was now the spiritual leader and chief overseer of the Episcopal Church of the largest country in Africa. Not only did I have to consider the spiritual and physical care of thousands upon thousands of people; I had to do so in a country that was still deeply wounded by civil war and where political and tribal tensions seethed just below the surface. My aim was to call people to God and to enable them to become self-reliant, free from poverty, and able to live in peace with each other. But in order to accomplish that end, some difficult and long-standing obstacles would have to be removed.

My people and I would have to overcome the tribal hostilities that had been part of the cultural landscape of South Sudan for so long. We would have to confront corruption in the government and even in the church. In order to bring about an environment where peace-loving Sudanese could build safe, satisfying lives, we had to call to account those who propagated violence and mistrust in order to further their own ends. I announced these priorities on the day of my enthronement, and they have been at the top of my agenda, every day since.

Wherever I go and whenever I have the opportunity, I tell anyone who will listen that tribalism, if left unchecked and unchallenged, is a cancer that will destroy South Sudan. Until Jieng, Nuer, Shilluk, Bari, Murle, and all other tribes of our land can live in peace, side by side, we will not be able to build a secure future for our children.

"If you are Jieng and want everything to be run by Jieng, that is bad," I tell them. "If you are Bari and want only Bari to be in charge, it is bad. Be proud of who you are as Jieng, Nuer, and all the rest, but don't believe that your tribe should dominate all others." I began preaching this message from the beginning, and I have not stopped since. I want everyone to know that we are all people of God, and God's purpose is to unite all his children together as one family.

Likewise, I have labored to make sure that our political leaders are accountable for their actions. For too long we have suffered under those who are mostly concerned with advancing their own agendas and gathering power unto themselves. In my remarks on the day of my enthronement, I urged my listeners "to respect yourselves, your government, and the country … Listen to God and pray for prosperity, love, and peace, while keeping an eye on those who may wish to fail us."[2]

As I took up my work as archbishop, I was determined to make it my business to "speak truth to power," as the leaders of the American Civil Rights Movement said. Although my chief goals were to work for peace and reconciliation for my country and people, I knew that without justice, there could be no lasting peace. And so, as primate of the church, I resolved to work for justice. It is a struggle that has continued until this very day.

❖ ❖ ❖

I concluded that the most efficient way to begin providing the fruits of peace and reconciliation to the people of South Sudan was to empower and equip as many as possible to take up this work in their own communities. To accomplish this, I initiated widespread programs of training for clergy, youth, and women, especially in the fields of religious ministry and education. I also set about training and equipping a corps of ambassadors for peace and reconciliation. I instituted programs of training in evangelism, good agricultural practices, and other practical topics that could immediately begin to improve the lives of my people. The number of dioceses grew from twenty-four to forty-six. We saw great improvements in communication and especially in education, as we organized some 300 schools in the country. We also established a health care organization, as we set up a large number of clinics.

I appealed to the Christians of Sudan and South Sudan to recommit to tithing, in order that the church would have the financial means to carry out needed programs. I also began a review of the nationwide theological and ministerial training programs with a view to establishing three additional seminaries and providing them with adequate faculty and staff. My vision was to renovate the existing hospital in Lui—which had been built in 1930—and also to build hospitals in Juba, Malakal, Rumbek, the Nuba Mountains, and Blue Nile State. We are still working to achieve this goal. We also focused on the need for more schools in various dioceses and for providing needed transportation infrastructure, such as trucks and river transports, for the use and work of the churches. Considering the successes with cultivating crops I had witnessed in Renk Diocese, we also began looking into acquiring agricultural properties for the church in Central and Western Equatoria, Yei, Upper Nile, Bahr el Ghazal, the Nuba Mountains, and Blue Nile State. We began constructing guest houses that the churches could use to get rental income, and we made plans for pharmacy centers in the dioceses, so that critical medicines could be distributed as efficiently as possible.

We began assessing the desperate need for assisting the millions of persons displaced by the war, including the thousands of "Lost Boys" who had been forced out of their homes during the decades-long conflict. Most of the lost boys were coming back from refugee camps in neighboring countries, especially the huge Kakuma refugee camp in Kenya. After the signing of the CPA—and we would witness this to an even greater degree with the passage of the 2011 independence referendum—the church was overwhelmed by all the people coming back at once. The ECS Sudan Development Relief Agency (SUDRA) was able to help resettle many people coming back, providing sorely needed assistance with food, clothing, and other needs. The church acted as a sort of transitional facility: a place people could go when they left the refugee camps to be reintroduced into everyday life in the country they had fled. Overall, our aim was to rehabilitate, reconstruct, and redevelop, so that South Sudanese could begin to rebuild their lives.

◈ ◈ ◈

Looming before all of us in the south, of course, was the referendum on southern independence, one of the central conditions of the Comprehensive Peace Agreement. The referendum was to take place in 2011, only three short years away. And in that time, a massive public education effort had to take place. Once again, the Christian churches of Sudan would shoulder the lion's share of the responsibility for seeing that the task was accomplished.

Many have reflected on why Khartoum not only allowed, but helped to facilitate the independence referendum for South Sudan. It is important to understand, first of all, that this was not the unified will of the entire northern political apparatus. President Bashir had many who bitterly opposed southern independence; it was by no means the unanimous desire of the northern leaders to offer the south such an opportunity.

However, several factors led Bashir and others to accept—even if grudgingly—the necessity of the independence referendum for the south. First, their military situation had been steadily deteriorating for some time. Under the unifying leadership of John Garang, the SPLA had been making steady gains against incursions by the forces of the Khartoum government. Additionally, the uprisings in Darfur had further destabilized the position of the central government. Finally, the war was costing Khartoum a great deal of oil revenue, since it prevented the rich fields in the south from being exploited.

But perhaps a major factor was the north's miscalculation of the south's ability to truly stand on its own feet. After all, for decades upon decades, the north had been able to play the southern tribal groups off against each other by utilizing tribal mistrust and, sometimes, by secretly arming one tribal group against another. Indeed, following the Addis Ababa Accords of 1972, the north had progressively ignored those provisions it found inconvenient, believing that its superior military power and organization permitted it to do as it liked. This, of course, led directly to the Second Civil War.

It is likely that many in the north believed that the independence referendum could either be stalled indefinitely or modified in ways that would be advantageous to the north. Or perhaps some believed that the south would inevitably fail to thrive as an independent state, and it would simply be a matter of Khartoum moving back into the vacuum and resuming its centuries-long domination of the south.

But Khartoum miscalculated both the level of mistrust the south had for the central government and the depth of southern resolve. As the days and weeks passed and southerners began to lean more and more decidedly toward independence from the north, the degree of Khartoum's misunderstanding became ever more clear.[3]

One of the reasons events developed this way, of course, was because of the monumental efforts undertaken by the south—largely led by the churches—to make certain that the people knew the provisions of the referendum, knew what was at stake, and knew what they had to do to make their voices heard. Thousands of people labored tirelessly, quite literally day and night, in order to see that the message reached virtually every person in South Sudan who would be eligible to vote in the coming referendum.

Bear in mind that all this was taking place in a country where the literacy rate is only about 27 percent. It was not as though we could simply put up billboards and send advertisements to the people of the south. Instead, we had to organize and conduct public meetings in every city neighborhood, town, and rural village that we could possibly reach. Over and over again, volunteers had to stand in front of the people and explain to them, point by point, the ramifications of the upcoming vote and its importance for South Sudan. We spoke in churches, we spoke in assembly halls, and we spoke in the shade of trees to people sitting on the ground.

It has been said that as the time for the referendum drew near, even people who could neither read nor write were able to recite most of the text of the referendum documents.[4] Certainly, we did everything possible to make sure that all of South Sudan was mobilized, registered, and ready to participate in the process of national self-determination. And yet, despite all this, there were problems and obstacles.

Khartoum, naturally, came to realize the likelihood that the majority of southern Sudanese would vote for independence. As this likelihood became more and more clear, they began employing tactics designed both to delay the referendum and also to pressure the new Government of South Sudan to back down from holding the vote at all. Various threats—some veiled and some rather open—surfaced in the national media about the fate of southerners living in the north, should the south vote to secede from the north. There was talk of the status of the region of Abyei, which lies on the line between north and south. Many northern elements wanted to settle this before the referendum could proceed— a tactic perceived by most in the south as no more than an attempt at delay. There were even military threats, with Khartoum massing its best-trained and most heavily armed troops on the border, near the oil fields.

As if all this were not bad enough, we also soon began to learn that the international community was having doubts about both the legitimacy and even the possibility of the national referendum. No doubt, the anti-referendum propaganda from Khartoum was having some effect in persuading world leaders that the people of South Sudan were incapable of self-determination. "They are tribal," the line went. "They will kill each other; only the strong hand of Khartoum can prevent anarchy in South Sudan." Such were the messages that came from the north in its campaign to discredit the referendum.

Those of us in the leadership of the churches of South Sudan realized that a major diplomatic effort was needed in order to present the accurate situation to the rest of the world, both to maintain pressure on Khartoum to permit the referendum to go forward, and also to insure that the necessary international resources would be made available to South Sudan in order to allow the referendum to be carried out successfully.

The general secretary of the Sudan Council of Churches, Rev. Dr. Ramadan Chan Liol, called together a council of church leaders to consider how to respond. After due deliberation, the council appointed a delegation to call upon world leaders. In addition to myself, the other members were: Paride Taban, Bishop Emeritus of the Catholic Church; Daniel Adwok Kur, also a bishop of the Catholic Church; and Rev. Dr. Chan Liol. An advisory team was also appointed that included His Excellency Dr. Sam Kobia, Special Envoy to Sudan; John Ashworth, advisor to the Sudan Council of Churches; and Mr. Rocco Blume of the Christian Aid organization.

We realized that many in the European Union, and perhaps even some in the office of the Secretary General of the United Nations, doubted the efficacy of the referendum. We were also very worried that without sufficient world attention, the referendum would be subverted, and would be neither free nor fair.

Accordingly, we divided the team in two parts, one to go the United Kingdom, and the other bound for the United States. Our purpose was to meet with as many opinion leaders as possible in order to get our concerns adequately heard and acted upon. I traveled with the UK team.

In a January 11, 2010, letter to the British prime minister at that time, Gordon Brown, I wrote,

> The peace process in Sudan has reached a critical point. With less than four months before National Elections and one year to the referendum on southern self-determination, the Comprehensive Peace Agreement (CPA) is on the brink of collapse....
>
> I am therefore visiting London to speak to you on behalf of the Episcopal Church of the Sudan (ECS), calling upon Her Majesty's Government, as a guarantor signatory of the CPA, to put more pressure on the NCP [National Congress Party, the governing political party of the Khartoum government] and SPLM [Sudanese People's Liberation Movement] to shore up the goal of a lasting peace in Sudan, peace which is currently so critically in the balance....

The Church proclaims, "Let my people choose," and urges renewed international focus on the political processes of the elections and the referendum, the latter of which must be considered inviolable. The Church supports the right of every individual Sudanese to have a free and fair say in the future of Sudan ... Sudan is in very real danger of descending back into a war which will not harm the elites and the politicians, but which will again destroy the lives of the voiceless mass of citizens for which I, on behalf of the Church, have journeyed to London to cry to the world....[5]

In response, I received from Mr. Brown a letter dated February 8, 2010, which said, in part,

The British Government is strongly committed to supporting all parties in Sudan in this effort. I remain personally committed to doing all I can to promote peace in Sudan. The UK Minister for Africa, Glenys Kinnock, visited Sudan on 11–13 January and underlined our support and desire for progress....

The consequences of a return to war are grave. However, I believe that lasting peace in Sudan is attainable and the UK will continue to work vigorously to that end.... Your work towards peace continues to make a real difference and I hope you will stay in close touch with us on your efforts during this crucial year.[6]

With Rocco Blume, I went again to London, October 3–8, 2010, where I warned all who would listen that such a delay in the referendum—and certainly any open attempt to halt it—would almost surely lead to the renewal of war in Sudan. I called upon world leaders to continue paying attention to what was happening in our country. "Come the ninth of January [2011], if nothing happens, people will go back to war; that is our fear," I said. In a news conference with the Archbishop of Canterbury at that time, the Most Reverend Rowan Williams, I urged world leaders to do all possible to insure that the vote took place on time. "I think the international community has an obligation to make sure the referendum is done," I said.[7] While I was there, I also met with members of the South Sudanese diaspora who were living in and near London. I urged them to do all possible to support the upcoming referendum. I addressed the conference of the Conservative Party of the United Kingdom, and I also met with Henry Bellingham, the British government's minister for Africa; Sir Peter Ricketts, the national security advisor for the United Kingdom; and many other government leaders with a special interest in African affairs. My visit in the UK was very well covered by the press, including reports on BBC Radio 4, BBC World Service, Al Jazeera television, the *Times of London*, the *Financial Times*, the *London Daily Telegraph*, and *Christianity Today*. I received strong assurances, from the Prime Minister and others, that the United Kingdom would support the right of self-determination for the people of South Sudan.

On October 10, 2010, I flew to New York to join the other team. They had been working in Indiana, Baltimore, and Washington, DC. In New York we met with UN Secretary General Ban Ki Moon. Once again, we presented to the secretary general our urgent case: it was necessary for the referendum to go forward, and it was essential that the world community work to help us ensure that it was conducted in a free and fair manner. Additionally, we alerted Secretary General Moon that pressures coming from Khartoum to settle differences about certain disputed territories as a condition of allowing the referendum to proceed were merely a stalling tactic designed, ultimately, to derail the referendum and pitch South Sudan into war, once again. So many times in the past, we told him, agreements were not honored. Because of this, the people of South Sudan had little confidence in any agreement coming out of Khartoum. "We appeal to the international community to stand united behind the terms of the Comprehensive Peace Agreement, which authorizes the referendum," we said.

One of the objectives of our team of emissaries was to convince the international community that the national referendum was much more than a simple technical, legal, or political exercise; it arose instead from the fundamental right of self-determination for the people of South Sudan. Further, we asserted that an outcome that reflected and respected the will of the people of South Sudan was more important than the sum of the technical procedures. "We have come to ring alarm bells," I told them. My message was that our communication of the many threats assembling to oppose the vote and the referendum should be heeded. We brought the warning so that later, no one would be able to say, "We didn't know."

While we were in New York, we also met with representatives of the governments of Belgium and Mexico, the Office for the Coordination of Humanitarian Affairs (OCHA), and many other world leaders, including the Holy See's permanent observer mission to the UN, the African Union Mission to the UN, and also the United Kingdom Mission to the UN. We called for international monitors to oversee the referendum process, including the polling places—both in the north and the south—to ensure fairness. I also had the opportunity to preach at Trinity Church, on Wall Street, and afterward to participate in a forum with church members. We left no stone unturned in our efforts to bring world attention to this crucial moment in Sudanese history. When we left to return home, all the members of our delegation felt confident that our pleas had been heard. We had great hope that world opinion would turn against the efforts of the northern government to subvert the referendum and cast doubt on its outcome.

Of course, to my great sorrow, not all the obstacles to the referendum came from Khartoum.

❖ ❖ ❖

Gen. George Athor Deng was a lieutenant general in the SPLA, which he joined in 1983. He rose up through the ranks to command the Jonglei Division before his promotion to Deputy Chief of Staff for Political and

Moral Orientation. As matters would prove, he was not a good political leader, and his morality was also sometimes called into question. He was widely rumored to be involved in weapons trafficking, influence peddling, and misappropriation of funds, both in Jonglei and Upper Nile States.

In April 2010, Athor had lost in an election for governor of Jonglei State. Unwilling to accept this result, he alleged fraud as the reason for his defeat, and eventually led a series of attacks on SPLA forces, leading to widespread insecurity and displacement of persons in the northwestern part of Jonglei State. General Athor declared himself the leader of the "South Sudan Democratic Movement" and its military wing, the "South Sudan Army." He held himself to be at war with the SPLA and the duly appointed Government of South Sudan. And all this was happening as time drew ever nearer for the independence referendum, scheduled for January 2011. I was devastated by this development, especially since Athor's actions could be held up by Khartoum as an example of one of their allegations: that South Sudan was incapable of exercising self-rule and would inevitably descend into internal infighting and chaos.

In an effort to bring an end to the violence and disastrous dissension, Salva Kiir Mayardit, at that time First Vice President of Sudan and President of the Government of South Sudan, made an urgent appeal to General Athor and his forces on October 6, 2010, going so far as to offer an executive pardon on the condition that they would lay down their arms and reintegrate with the SPLA. But Athor refused this generous offer, declining even to reveal his whereabouts, not to mention accepting the terms of the presidential pardon.

President Kiir's next action was to appoint a High-Level Committee for Reconciliation on November 30, 2010, with me as chair. I was only too glad to accept the responsibility, knowing that through many years of conflict and difficulty, the churches of Sudan, and especially the Episcopal Church, had fostered a well-deserved reputation for working toward justice and reconciliation.

Joining me on this vital committee were Bishop Rudolf Deng Majak from Wau Diocese of the Roman Catholic Church; Rev. Tijwok Aguet, Presidential Advisor for Religious Affairs; Lt. Gen. Dr. Majak D'Agot Atem, head of national security for the Government of South Sudan; and Lt. Gen. Ayuen Alier, Deputy Chief of Staff of the SPLA. We went to Malakal and from there went to the village of Khorflus to meet with the people in the surrounding area, who urged us to bring an end to the humanitarian crisis being created by Athor's uprising. The next day, we met with the people of Atar, another small town, who also begged us to seek a ceasefire and reconciliation between the warring groups. Further, they assured us that the unrest was due solely to competing political ambitions among leaders in the SPLM and SPLA that had emerged during the previous elections.

Next, we made efforts to contact General Athor and gain his assurances of safe conduct in order to meet with him. We were able to go to his secret base on December 16, less than a month before the referendum on national independence was to take place. Unless we were successful at ending this conflict, a huge percentage of the population of northern Jonglei and southern Upper Nile States would be unable to go to the polls, which would be a national travesty.

We met with him for most of the day, urging him to accept the presidential pardon, disarm his troops, and rejoin the SPLA. While we were there, General Athor's phone rang. He spoke with one of his field commanders and then informed us that a unit of the SPLA government troops was moving toward our location. He said that they were only two or three miles away and were being held back by his forces.

We were very surprised and deeply troubled by this news, because we were there under orders from President Kiir, and the SPLA should have been made well aware of our presence and our mission. This was not the right time for an SPLA attack on General Athor's forces, especially since the committee that was trying to create peace was now potentially caught in the crossfire!

Somehow, Athor's headquarters area did not come under direct attack,

---

and when we had concluded our meeting, he permitted us to return to Malakal. This alone was rather remarkable; we fully expected that we might be held as hostages. But apparently God touched the heart of General Athor, and we made it safely back to Malakal. Indeed, only two days after this, a battle between Athor's forces and the SPLA claimed the lives of twenty soldiers. The fighting made it much more difficult to negotiate the next meeting, but we were able to continue our talks with General Athor.

At one point, I went back to him secretly, accompanied by Rev. James Partab (leader of the evangelical Presbyterians) and asked him, "Are you fighting the people of South Sudan or the government?"

"I am fighting the government, not the people of South Sudan," he told me.

"But please, General, if you are not fighting the people of South Sudan will you not allow them to vote for the referendum to decide their future? Why will you take their voice away from them because of your dissatisfaction?"

With many more imploring words such as these, we continued to persuade General Athor to stop obstructing this great moment in the history of our country. Subsequently, we brought both sides to the table and were able to witness the signing of a ceasefire between Athor and the SPLA on January 5, 2011—a scant four days before the national referendum.[8]

Apparently, as we would learn later, General Athor had originally broached the idea of having the Church mediate the conflict, believing that the presence of one or more religious leaders would guarantee openness and sincerity on both sides. Certainly, mistrust was rampant throughout our country at this time. In fact, this would not be the last time I would have to confront this entrenched adversary of unity for my country.

❖ ❖ ❖

The referendum on the independence of South Sudan took place on schedule, January 9–15, 2011. Southerners who lived in Darfur also voted, and southern Sudanese in Australia, Canada, Egypt, Ethiopia, Kenya, Uganda, the United Kingdom, and the United States also cast ballots. At least five international agencies observed the polling, with representatives that included former US President Jimmy Carter, former UN Secretary General Kofi Annan, and then–US Senator John Kerry. The African Union, the European Union, the League of Arab States, and the Intergovernmental Authority on Development, in addition to a number of Sudanese nongovernmental organizations, also monitored the referendum. More than 97 percent of persons registered to vote participated in the referendum, and the final vote was 98.83 percent in favor of independence.

With this historic vote and ratification on the following July 9, South Sudan became the world's newest nation. Now, it would be up to us to learn how to become a unified people. This would not be an easy lesson to master.

❖ ❖ ❖

In 2012 I was deeply honored to be nominated, along with three other entities, for the Chatham House Prize, an annual award presented by the Royal Institute of International Affairs ("Chatham House") in London to "the statesperson or organisation deemed by Chatham House members to have made the most significant contribution to the improvement of international relations in the previous year."[9]

The Royal Institute of International Affairs, with its headquarters in the historic Chatham House building on St. James's Square, is one of the world's leading organizations devoted to the study, analysis, and promotion of understanding of major international issues and foreign affairs. A sister institution to the US Council on Foreign Relations, Chatham House, as it is usually called, is one of the most influential "think tanks" in the world, according to numerous academic institutions and foreign policy experts.

I was nominated because of my efforts for peace and reconciliation in Sudan and South Sudan, especially following the end of the Second Civil

War and South Sudanese independence. My leadership of the initiatives that resulted in the ceasefire between General Athor and the SPLA was especially noted, since this enabled all of South Sudan to go the polls for the national referendum without fear of violence.

Nominated along with me were others whose leadership in the midst of pivotal world events was of incalculable benefit to humanity. Christine Lagarde, who managed the International Monetary Fund during the world financial crisis of 2011, was nominated for her steady leadership in seeking solutions to the crisis and stabilizing world financial systems. Jonas Gahr Støre, Norwegian minister of foreign affairs, was nominated for his guidance in disarmament issues and in policies related to the Arctic, as well as his help in orchestrating the national response to the vicious attacks on Norwegians by a lone wolf terrorist in 2011. Finally, Sheikh Rached Ghannouchi, leader of the Ennahdha Party, and Dr. Moncef Marzouki, president of Tunisia, were jointly nominated for their successful efforts at compromise during Tunisia's dramatic democratic transition of 2011. Ultimately, the Chatham House Prize for 2012 was bestowed on Ghannouchi and Marzouki.

Nevertheless, to be nominated with other such distinguished world leaders was one of the great honors of my life. I accepted this recognition, not so much for myself, but more on behalf of the people of South Sudan. This was an important platform on which the world had the opportunity to see our new nation and to understand a bit more of its needs and aspirations.

1. Matthew Davies, "Sudan's New Primate, Archbishop Daniel Deng Bul, Enthroned in Juba Cathedral." Anglican Communion News Service, April 22, 2008 [online]. Available at http://www.anglicannews.org/news/2008/04/sudans-new-primate,-archbishop-daniel-deng-bul-enthroned-in-juba-cathedral.aspx (accessed October 3, 2016).
2. Ibid.
3. See also Natsios, *Sudan, South Sudan, and Darfur*, 190–92.

4. Natsios, private interview, November 25, 2015.

5. "Appeal to Her Majesty's Government," letter from Archbishop Daniel Deng Bul Yak to Rt. Hon. Gordon Brown, MP. January 11, 2010. Papers of Archbishop Daniel Deng Bul Yak.

6. Letter from Rt. Hon. Gordon Brown, MP, to Archbishop Daniel Deng Bul Yak. February 8, 2010. Papers of Archbishop Daniel Deng Bul Yak.

7. Michael Holden, "Archbishop Warns Vote Failure Will Restart Sudan War." Reuters, October 7, 2010 [online]. Available at http://www.reuters.com/article/us-sudan-archbishop-idUSTRE6962LA20101007 (accessed October 4, 2016).

8. See also Haru Mutasa, "Sudan's SPLA Signs Pact with Rebels." *Al Jazeera* (English), January 6, 2011. Available at http://www.aljazeera.com/video/africa/2011/01/2011168020395407.html (accessed October 5, 2016).

9. "Chatham House Prize." Chatham House (Royal Institute of International Affairs) [online]. Available at https://www.chathamhouse.org/chatham-house-prize (accessed October 8, 2016).

CHAPTER 10

Fighting for Peace in the World's Newest Nation

I wish with all my heart that the trouble with General Athor, just before the national referendum on independence in 2011, had been the final obstacle to peace and unity in the new nation of South Sudan. However, this would prove not to be the case. In fact, in many tragic ways, the dissension between Athor and the leadership of the Government of South Sudan and the SPLA would prove to be an ominous harbinger of things to come.

I sometimes think with deep regret of the untimely death of John Garang. In late July 2005, less than a month after he and President Bashir signed the agreements that officially brought an end to the Second Civil War and also made Dr. Garang First Vice President of Sudan and President of the Government of South Sudan, he died in a helicopter crash near the Kenya-Uganda border. The investigation committee that was established following Garang's death has not, to date, officially released the details of their inquiry into the crash. However, the incident has been officially blamed on pilot error, and that cause seems to have been accepted by most, over time.

But with the death of this charismatic and visionary leader, rivalries within the SPLA and SPLM suddenly had greater scope for activity. It is a sad fact that where the opportunity for power exists, people with great ambitions will contend—even violently—to control that power. That is what led to the rebellion of General Athor, when he lost the gubernatorial election in Jonglei State, and that same lust for power lies at the root of most of the ongoing dangers still faced by our very young nation.

I have dedicated my ministry as Archbishop and Primate to confronting this dangerous desire for power. The overriding goal of my life, as a spiritual leader of the people of South Sudan, is to foster a climate of peaceful coexistence and mutual respect among the various peoples of South Sudan. Only when we are able to settle our differences peacefully and in an atmosphere of trust will we be able to build a secure future for our children and grandchildren.

Sadly, though, my nation and its people have had very little experience with peaceful coexistence, especially for the last sixty years. To cultivate peace in South Sudan at this time in history is to labor in a field that is choked with weeds of mistrust that have been growing for a very long time and that have spread their poisonous seeds far and wide.

❖ ❖ ❖

On Maundy Thursday in March 2011, very shortly after the national referendum, I traveled to my home county, Twic East, in Jonglei State. I went there to celebrate Easter and the resurrection of our Lord with the Christians in Twic East County, of course. But I also traveled there, in the company of my fellow bishops, to resolve an inter-clan conflict that had become violent.

I was going to Twic East also under the aegis of the newly created Presidential Committee for Community Peace, Reconciliation, and Tolerance in Jonglei State (PCCPRT), which President Salva Kiir had asked me to chair. Our charge was to go to the counties and smaller political subdivisions (*payams,* which are in turn made up of *bomas*) of Jonglei State and to engage with youth, women, and church leaders along with the county commissioners, local government administrators, paramount chiefs, head chiefs, national and state legislators, and others in order to foster peaceful coexistence among the tribes and clans of the region. We would set up meetings and conferences in which we would call together those who were in conflict with each other, urging them toward dialogue, rather than fighting, as a way to work through their disputes.

With me on this mission of peace to Twic East were Rt. Rev. Joseph Garang, Bishop of Renk Diocese; Rt. Rev. Micah Laila, Bishop of Terekeka; Rt. Rev. Paul Yugusuk, Assistant Bishop of Lomega in the Diocese of Torit; and others. We were greeted by Bishop Ezekiel Diing, of Twic East, and other senior clergy, as well as Rebecca Nyandeng de Mabior, widow of John Garang, who owns a farm in the area. As spiritual leaders of the Christians in South Sudan, we were the first to come to the area in order to address the violence; no one from the government had been there, as at least one local chief told us.

The most serious problem we faced, as we called a community conference to focus on the issues troubling the area, was the conflict between two clans of Jieng, the Ayual and Dachuek. A dispute over grazing rights to a certain piece of land had escalated into inter-clan fighting on March 3 that had claimed the lives of twenty-one people in the village of Wanglei and had left an additional thirty-seven injured.

It is significant that the violence in Twic East County had arisen along kinship lines and for the same motivation that had so often sparked inter-tribal and inter-clan conflict for generations in South Sudan: grazing rights for cattle. During the decades of war, these tensions did not go away. Indeed, the devastation brought by the war, along with the usual cycles of drought, had only made the pressure worse on those trying to maintain their traditional, agrarian way of life. When people are hungry, and when they see their cattle dying, they will fight in order to survive. They will steal cattle. And it will not matter to them whom they are victimizing, if they believe that they must take such actions in order to survive. Furthermore, with Khartoum sowing even more mistrust among the tribes and clans—and often supplying weapons to the combatants—the potential for inter-ethnic violence was, in some ways, higher than ever.

These were the types of conflicts we were dealing with as our nation was being born. Yes, we had achieved independence from Khartoum. But now, we had to learn how to live together as fellow citizens, instead of continuing to think of each other as just another type of enemy.

We met for some six hours of intense discussion and negotiation with community leaders, seeking solutions to the causes of division. The principal accomplishment of that meeting was the appointment of a committee to facilitate face-to-face meetings between the leaders of the Ayual and Dachuek clans.

❖❖❖

Later that year, after witnessing more violence among the people of Jonglei State, I traveled to Bor, the capital of Jonglei, under a mandate from leaders of communities all across the state, to address the Jonglei State legislative assembly. Skirmishes and outright battles were erupting everywhere, it seemed, and the Murle and Luo Nuer people appeared locked in a particularly implacable conflict. On October 7, 2011, I began my address to the Jonglei parliament with the quotation of Psalm 133:1, which says, "How good and pleasant it is when God's people live together in unity."

But Jonglei was not unified—far from it. I reminded them, however, that harmony does not require everyone to sing precisely the same note; it only requires that the various notes blend in a way that benefits the whole. "But we must agree on our purpose in life: to work together for God and Nation. And the Church has always nurtured peaceful coexistence. History is replete with examples of how the church has helped civilization to avert self-extermination and turn to peace."

I recalled for the assembled lawmakers the many ways that the Church and its leaders had worked to promote peace and justice, beginning with Archbishop Tutu in the struggle against apartheid, and referencing other great leaders in history—Martin Luther King Jr., William Wilberforce, Pope John Paul II, and others—who used their platforms within the Church to call tirelessly for changes in society that were necessary in order for God's purpose to be served and for human lives to be saved. I also mentioned the recent accords reached with Khartoum that had permitted our nation its opportunity for self-determination. I reminded them that truly visionary leadership, like that personified by our late leader, John Garang, has the ability to step back from personal demands in order to create space for reason to prevail. But at that moment, in places throughout the state, reason was being trampled by hatred and violence.

"Jonglei is on fire," I told them. "When one thinks about the many lives our people lost fighting a just war, the war for self-determination, this latest twist of events would surely make one sick. It makes a mockery of our independence. It abuses the martyrs of this great nation. It says they died in vain."[1]

I called on the lawmakers to take up the cause of their people in their time of deep need. I relayed to them the anguished cries of the Luo Nuer and Murle to whom I had spoken, characterized by the following twelve urgent priorities:

1. Stop the war;
2. Demand that political leaders stop inciting violence between people groups;
3. Begin dialogue;
4. Let the Church partner with the government in bringing about stability;
5. Put in place the necessary communications infrastructure;
6. Increase security forces;
7. Address rampant unemployment;
8. Rebuild damaged medical facilities and systems;
9. Disarm all civilians;
10. Monitor the borders, especially for arms trafficking;
11. Apply justice fairly to all;
12. Include all stakeholders in the process.

During my time with the lawmakers, we developed a plan for bringing together Luo Nuer and Murle leaders from among the legislative assembly as a means of beginning productive dialogue between the two factions.

Additionally, we put in place plans for meetings among the various communities in Jonglei State, including all six major tribal groups, so that their concerns and needs could be determined and a plan of action developed.

I continued working on the ground together with the Sudan Council of Churches and assisted by other heads of local churches such as Archbishop Paulino Lukudu Loro of Juba Catholic Archdiocese, Bishop Arkanjero Wani, Presiding Bishop of Africa Inland Church, Bishop Michael Taban Toro, Chairman of Sudan Council of Churches, and Rev. Mark Akec Cien, Acting Secretary of Sudan Council of Churches. We called on the people of Jonglei to fulfill the mandate of Jesus, who promised in the Gospel of St. John, chapter 14, verse 27, "My peace I leave with you": a peace that cannot be maintained by military force, but only by recognition of the dignity and worth of each person, accompanied by willingness to forgive and practice reconciliation. This need was tragically evident during the Christmas season of 2011, when widespread bloodshed occurred. During this same time period, in fact, Gen. George Athor, who had unfortunately backed away from his commitment to peace since agreeing to the ceasefire in January, died violently. He was attempting to cross into Morobo County, which borders both Uganda and the Democratic Republic of Congo, on an apparent trip to recruit fighters, when he was killed in a battle with South Sudan border guards, according to the government spokesman.

We learned that the Murle people were widely regarded as principal perpetrators of attacks on other groups. These attacks, of course, typically occasioned retaliatory actions, both from Luo Nuer and Jieng, who were also being drawn into the conflict. Luo Nuer youth, in particular, felt justified in retaliating, in the absence of sufficient government security forces to keep order. In fact, we realized a severe disconnect between the young men in the kraals and other remote places and their political and village leaders. In order to salvage any chance at durable peace, we had to come up with a way to effectively engage these young people.

To make matters worse, the many years of civil war and widespread militarization of the countryside meant that more advanced weapons were available in greater quantity. Conflict in the country had moved far beyond traditional, small-scale cattle raiding; it now involved more sophisticated tactics, more deadly weapons, and more military training. Needless to say, all this had dire implications for the escalation of violence.

Nevertheless, we labored continuously to spread the message: "The peace process has not failed, because peace cannot be allowed to fail." As the government pursued a track of suppression and disarmament, we determined to pursue a parallel grassroots track of mobilization for peace, based on our earlier "people-to-people" initiatives. We began conducting "peace workshops" in villages across Jonglei State, identifying those who could be trained as "peace mobilizers" in their communities. We went out to the cattle camps and met face-to-face with the young men there, urging them to return to the traditional values of respect for and obedience to elders and chiefs. We reached out to non-governmental organizations (NGOs), urging them to continue doing all they could to support the peace process by affording humanitarian aid and infrastructure improvement, and above all by applying their efforts fairly and equitably, in a way that would not exacerbate underlying tensions. We appealed to the South Sudanese diaspora to cease any communication that could heighten enmities or encourage violent solutions to disagreements. We further encouraged South Sudanese citizens to stop believing every rumor involving alleged nefarious actions by other tribal groups. Instead, we urged, people should be critical of what they heard and should weigh their responses carefully. Finally, we insisted that all parties must accept accountability for their own actions and reactions. No longer could we afford for people or groups to blame their violence on the violence committed by others.

❖ ❖ ❖

It became clear that we needed to make a broad, sweeping attempt to bring together people of all constituencies, communities, and concerns in order to promote dialogue that could lead to peace. We had to begin convincing people that negotiation, not violence, was the way to settle differences. As one way of promoting such dialogue, I convened the All-Jonglei Communities Conference, May 1–5, 2012, in Bor. We called together government officials, tribal leaders, women, and youth from all eleven counties of Jonglei State and met together to hear each other's concerns before working together to develop strategies for addressing them.

In our discussions, several issues quickly rose to the surface. It soon became clear that if we did not begin to address these problems facing the people of Jonglei State, there could be no hope for long-lasting peace in the communities there.

Underdevelopment. Comments from people living in the remote areas of the state made it clear that we had a problem with favoritism in the allocation of government resources available for maintaining and improving such basic necessities as roads, schools, telecommunications facilities, healthcare, and even reliable access to clean water. If people do not have these most basic elements necessary to sustain life, it is useless to talk to them about such high concepts as reconciliation, forgiveness, and mutual respect. As it is sometimes said, "When you cannot breathe, nothing else matters." It is the same for people who cannot get life-sustaining water, or who have no way to transport their crops to market or to trade for things they need.

We developed a plan for more effectively approaching the federal and state government about doing their share to address these concerns. We also identified non-governmental organizations (NGOs), both domestic and international, that could be approached to help with funding infrastructure improvements for the people of Jonglei State.

Unemployment. When people—and especially young men—have no means of earning a living, they will follow anyone who promises regular food and wages. Indeed, the refugee camps in Kenya and Uganda were fertile recruitment grounds, not only for the SPLA, but also for the semi-official and even renegade militia leaders who thrived on the chaos of the civil war as a way to further their own private ambitions. In some cases, the cattle camps of South Sudan were becoming little more than bases of operation for various militia commanders, many of whom utilized tribal rivalries to insure the loyalty of their followers as they carried out extortions, protection schemes, human and weapons trafficking, and other nefarious undertakings.

We called for the creation of income-generating projects—such as the rental properties and agricultural operations the church had carried out in Renk Diocese and which we were now deploying in other places—to provide opportunity for people to earn an honest living. We laid out the framework for equitable employment practices and, again, identified the governmental and non-governmental entities that would have a vested or demonstrated interest in coming alongside our people to help us get our initiatives up to speed.

Trauma. Sudanese my age and younger had scarcely known a time during the last five decades when the country had not been locked in civil strife of one type or another. Additionally, natural disasters such as drought and flood, along with the rampant disease that inevitably accompanies widespread dislocation, had winnowed our people mercilessly for so many years.

The conference developed plans for extending community counseling services across Jonglei State and making them readily available to as many people as possible. Additionally, we noted that the creation of suitable living conditions would be one of the most important steps in helping people normalize their lives and create around themselves the space they needed for healing. We affirmed the vital importance of engaging our youth in productive and profitable activities, such as organized sports and especially religious and moral training and instruction. If we intended to break the cycle of poverty, desperation, and violence, we realized that we had to teach our young people how to be better friends, employees, fellow workers, and citizens.

Abduction of women, girls, and boys. Many of these women and young girls were being trafficked into the slave market and sold as "wives." The boys were being forced into slave labor, usually caring for their captors' cattle. These poor souls were often being used as "payment" for militia members, and they were frequently subjected to rape, other forms of violence, and even vicious murders.

First, we called on the government to enforce the laws that exist to prohibit such barbarism. We beseeched our national and state leaders to arrest and prosecute those accused of such horrible crimes, and to subject those found guilty to the most severe punishment. We called for the return of the abductees wherever possible, and in cases where that was not possible for some reason, we laid out guidelines for the status of these women and boys to become regularized by negotiation so that they have the same rights and privileges as any other citizen of South Sudan. At a minimum, we wished for them to become oriented to the local culture and way of life and to be considered as part of the community that had taken them—not as slaves. After the Jonglei conference it was stated that women and boys had to be returned to their homes, and this happened in many cases. We also called for better and more accurate registration of births and marriages, so that the identities of persons are easier to document and validate.

Cattle theft. This problem alone accounted for much of the general instability and mistrust among the people of Jonglei State. Given the centrality of cattle raising, not only in South Sudanese culture, but also to the basic ability of persons in my country to feed themselves and their families, any threat to a community's cattle strikes at its most essential identity. And, as we saw with the Jieng, Luo Nuer, and Murle, rivalries over cattle can arise, not only between different tribes, but sometimes also between different clans of the same tribe.

To further complicate the problem, organized gangs of cattle rustlers also are known to victimize rural communities. Sometimes, SPLA deserters, either desperate for means of sustenance or else simply committed to a criminal life, engage in cattle theft. Finally, young men who want to marry will sometimes steal cattle in order to meet the increasingly steep bride prices demanded by fathers and village elders.

To meet these challenges, our conference first recommended the formation of units with the sole responsibility of investigating and preventing stock theft. We requested that additional police forces be deployed throughout Jonglei State, and especially in areas where cattle theft was rampant. We called for better regulation of the borders between payams, counties, and other states, and we petitioned the government for aerial surveillance assets that could be used to help with patrolling the countryside. We also placed an increased responsibility on communities to police themselves. For example, if a young man has suddenly acquired cattle for a bride price when he had few cattle before, it is likely that someone in his village knows the source of his sudden wealth. We made it the responsibility of clan and village chiefs to uphold the law in their communities and to insist that their people obeyed the law, also. We outlined a plan for extending amnesty for certain instances of past cattle theft, in exchange for greater cooperation going forward. And finally, we called on local chiefs and elders to regulate the bride prices being demanded in their communities, as rampant "dowry inflation" was one of the underlying social pressures contributing greatly to the problem.

Incidentally, on May 20, 2012, in Bor, the Twic East County Commissioner, Dau Akoi Jurkuch, was able to announce the reconciliation of the Ayual and Dachuek clans, due to an initiative led by Rebecca Nyandeng, partly as an outgrowth of our meetings. Her efforts towards bringing peace between these two clans brought great blessing and increased stability to the area.[2]

Violence against elderly persons, women, and children. The wanton killing of vulnerable persons was a tragic outgrowth of the general lawlessness that was threatening to engulf Jonglei State. We insisted that culpable persons be arrested, tried, and, if convicted, severely punished. We affirmed that one of the most basic duties of any government is to protect its citizens, and we urged both federal and state authorities to carry out disarmament programs intended to take weapons out of the hands of armed insurgents or even tribal hotheads who might be inclined to commit violence against groups they considered their rivals. Once again, we discussed a program of amnesty to be considered for deaths resulting from the confusion and chaos of war, but we also called for compensation to the families of those who had been unjustly killed, once disarmament had been completed.

Armed insurgents. The rebellion of General Athor was not the only instance of individuals becoming disgruntled by the outcome of democratic processes and subsequently taking the law into their own hands. David Yau Yau, who had been the county secretary of the South Sudan Relief and Rehabilitation Commission for Pibor County, at that time in Jonglei State (now a part of Boma State), was a candidate in the April 2010 election for a seat in the Jonglei State Assembly. He lost the election by a wide margin but, like George Athor, he could not accept this outcome and accused the SPLA of voter intimidation and fraud. In May of that year, he led an armed clash with the SPLA. He signed a ceasefire agreement with Government of South Sudan (GoSS) in June 2011, but defected again in April 2012 to lead a predominantly Murle militia group, which he eventually dubbed the Cobra Faction of Athor's South Sudan Democratic Movement (SSDM).

Such militias, though purportedly organized to uphold "democracy," are generally no more than fronts for human and weapons trafficking, livestock theft, and other illegal activities that cause fear, regional instability, and spiraling cycles of violence. The only persons who benefit from such "democratic" organizations are the leaders who enrich themselves at the expense of their innocent victims.

Our conference recognized, first, the need to educate and sensitize the Murle people of the Pibor region to the tactics and motivations of David Yau Yau and others like him. We urged the government to intercede militarily to halt the trafficking of women and children and to set up effective buffer zones and aerial surveillance that could help the law-abiding people of Pibor County to continue rebuilding their lives. We called for improvement in roads and communications infrastructure, interdiction of sources for illegal weapons, and greater community awareness and self-policing. As a part of community self-empowerment, we also reached out to the cattle camp youth in order to educate them about the situation and to recruit their leaders into forces organized for protection of communities and community resources. We further generated a framework for greater inter-community cooperation and interaction, including sports activities, citizenship workshops and conferences, and consistent follow-up from community, church, and political leaders.

Prior to our Jonglei conference, the government had organized a meeting of chiefs in Bentiu. A number of resolutions and agreements were made at that conference that were signed by all the chiefs, and so at our Jonglei conference, we called participants' attention back to these Bentiu accords and urged the government to implement the resolutions that had been agreed to there.

Other issues. During the conference, we also discussed problems with food production in Jonglei State, which had been severely disrupted by all the instability; resettlement of the thousands upon thousands of internally displaced persons (IDPs), those who had been forced from their homes and farms because of the violence; various border disputes involving entities at the village, payam, state, and even international levels; administrative problems requiring the attention, intervention, and, in some cases, reform of local and state policies and procedures; and other regional matters concerning local authorities, infrastructure, and security.

At the end of the conference, we presented to President Kiir and other government officials our conclusions and resolutions in a document ending with the following statement:

We, the participants in the Conference, representing the six communities of Jonglei State:

- Commit ourselves to peace, reconciliation and tolerance amongst our communities.
- Commit ourselves to these Resolutions.
- Appeal to our national and state governments to assist and to ensure that they are implemented.

❖❖❖

Later that year, I met with the Speaker of the Jonglei State Legislative Assembly, Hon. Chol Wal, in Bor, to report on the progress of our many efforts to bring peace to Jonglei State. Attending with me were Bishop Ruben Akurdit Ngong of Bor Diocese, Episcopal Church of Sudan (ECS); Hon. Awol Gaijang Awol and Hon. Matthew Matiok, of the Jonglei parliament; and Rev. John Chol Daau, a former "Lost Boy" who subsequently became a priest in the ECS and founded the Good Shepherd College and Seminary in 2004.

We reviewed the mandate for the Committee for Community Peace, Reconciliation, and Tolerance in Jonglei, including its constitution earlier that year by President Kiir. We recounted our May conference involving six communities of Jonglei State, including the signing of the peace treaty among the six localities, in which they agreed to halt hostilities against each other.

We noted, however, that certain communities had not been represented at that conference and had not participated in our peace dialogues. Specifically, Paweny, Pigi, Twic East, and Pochalla Counties had unresolved issues that demanded the immediate attention of everyone concerned with the peace process. We informed the speaker that President Kiir, after reviewing our report, urged the committee to continue its work, with a specific focus on these counties where threats to peace remained.

As we shared with Speaker Wal, with the aid of Reverend John Chol Daau, along with Hon. Haruun Lual Run, and Hon. Anne Kimo—both members of the National Legislative Assembly—I undertook to meet with various government and community leaders in Pigi County to gain a better understanding of the problems there. I also wished to obtain commitments from them to put aside past grudges and grievances and to work earnestly for reconciliation.

❖ ❖ ❖

Perhaps this is a good place to emphasize something I said earlier about the historical influence of the Christian Church in South Sudan. It is probably difficult for a person reading these words who lives in, say, the United States or even Germany, to imagine that a government official would drop everything in order to come to a meeting with a church leader, even a high official in an ecclesiastical organization. In the West, the Church simply does not often command such respect or influence. But in South Sudan, when, as Archbishop of the Episcopal Church of Sudan and South Sudan, I request a meeting with a government official—even if it is the president of the country—I am not often refused. Because of its long history of working to provide basic educational, medical, social, and vocational infrastructure—in addition to its role in spiritual and ethical guidance—the Christian Church in South Sudan commands wide and deep respect and influence among the people. Government and military leaders know this, too, and when Church leaders speak, they are not usually ignored.

Certainly, this does not mean that matters in South Sudan always proceed in the way the Church would wish. People are fallible and subject to fear, anger, and ignorance. Government leaders are often swayed by their ambition for power instead of concern for their fellow citizens and respect for moral and ethical principles. Despite all this, however, the Church will never cease its efforts to bring peace, understanding, compassion, and justice to bear on the society that we are called to serve. In the Gospel of Matthew, chapter 5, and in many other places, Christ has commissioned us to be peacemakers; we can never lay aside this calling.

❖ ❖ ❖

In our further discussions with Speaker Wal, several participants noted that fuel for the ongoing conflagrations came from politicians, inciting various ethnic rivalries. In various ways and for various motives, certain leaders appeared unwilling to engage in authentic dialogue. All of us recognized that these persons had to be called to account, even if it required intervention from the highest authorities in the nation.

We also recognized that in many cases, we were still dealing with hostility instigated during the troubles with General Athor and his followers. Because of the fighting and killing between militia units and the SPLA, grudges remained, and old loyalties continued to obstruct progress toward reconciliation.

In the end, we agreed that, though progress was evident, much more remained to be done. We developed lists of community and government leaders in the affected areas and planned meetings that would bring together representatives of the rival groups for open dialogue and sharing of differences. These meetings would then be followed by community-wide gatherings for dissemination and discussion of the agreements and commitments of the leaders. Results of all these efforts would be compiled and presented to President Kiir for his evaluation and recommendations.

Bishop Akurdit stated the necessity of creating peace for the sake of our children and grandchildren. "It is unfortunate when children feel ashamed of the leadership of their forefathers," he said. "We must record a history of peace for the benefit of future generations … We must continue praying that peace will prevail … "[3]

❖ ❖ ❖

In March 2013, the subcommittee monitoring and working with various groups in counties with unresolved issues made its report to President Kiir and others. We noted that as a result of our work, attacks in Jonglei State had declined from a rate of about 140 per month to a single attack in July 2012 and two incidents in August 2012, as the subcommittee of the PCCPRT confirmed by monitoring the eleven counties of Jonglei State. We noted, however, that the activities of David Yau Yau and his rebels still posed a threat; indeed much of Pibor County had been in turmoil since

November 2012, when Yau Yau and his allied Murle youth had ramped up their aggressive activities, using advanced armaments likely obtained from entities based in Khartoum. Thus once again, the age-old pattern had reasserted itself: Khartoum taking advantage of southern rivalries to arm one side against the other, destabilizing both.

In 2013, David Yau Yau signed a second agreement with the government and became chief administrator of the Pibor area until the creation of twenty-eight states, at which time Boma became a state. At this time, he was appointed as deputy minister of defense.

In response, a program of community policing was being implemented. Though arming the population held many risks—especially in light of recent disarmament efforts carried out by the GoSS—this seemed the only way to enable communities to protect themselves against the depredations of Yau Yau and other renegade commanders. Accordingly, the governor of Jonglei State had authorized the county commissioners to organize community forces, consisting of forty young men from each *boma* who would be trained, uniformed, and armed to protect their communities. This was not an ideal solution, we conceded, but in light of how thinly the SPLA was stretched at that time by ongoing threats from Khartoum and also by the effort to contain and disarm David Yau Yau, it was the best solution that presented itself.

Naturally, Yau Yau's attacks were causing widespread dislocation in Bor and nearby counties, including waves of herders and others fleeing across the White Nile into Lake and Central Equatoria States, further disrupting communities there, as the refugees from violence tried to make a place for themselves. Others had fled into Bor Town or even to Juba, or else were simply squatting along the sides of the highway between Bor and Juba, hoping desperately for protection from the government.

Not surprisingly in such a chaotic and dangerous situation, many people in the affected communities were critical of government responses, both state and federal. Similarly, the reaction of the UN Mission (UNMISS) forces often left much to be desired, according to the victims, who even accused them, in some cases, of giving more favorable attention to Murle interests, to the detriment of others.

Our report noted another disturbing development that would soon come to have devastating consequences for our new nation. We reported that a group of individuals in a Duk County payam that borders Wunroor County were undertaking efforts to secede from Duk County and to join themselves with Wunroor County. Apparently, these persons had warned the governor of Jonglei State in a letter that they were taking this action and would proceed by force, if necessary. The most ominous part of this news was that these people had then gone to meet with the Vice President of the Republic of South Sudan, Riek Machar, to seek his support for their demands.

❖ ❖ ❖

This would not be the first time that Riek Machar's name was associated with unrest and division among South Sudanese political and military circles. In 1991, during the Second Sudanese Civil War, he fell into disagreement with John Garang and formed a splinter group of the Sudanese People's Liberation Army that he called SPLA/Nasir Faction, named after the so-called "Nasir Declaration" that preceded the schism. During this "rebellion within a rebellion," Machar's forces overran Twic East County, Bor County, and other locations in Jonglei State, spawning the violence that claimed the lives of my father-in-law, mother-in-law, and brother-in-law.

Eventually, Machar and Garang were reconciled, and at the end of the Second Civil War, Machar was brought into the Government of South Sudan as Vice President. No doubt, this was an attempt to forge a useful alliance between his faction and the main branches of the SPLA and SPLM, by that time led by President Salva Kiir. Ultimately, however, the underlying problems were never fully addressed, and this would become tragically apparent before many months had passed.

◈ ◈ ◈

It was clear to us that the conflict between Duk and Wunroor Counties, and likely other disagreements, were becoming politicized. While it is true that many of these troubles had their roots in tribal and clan rivalries, it is just as true that ambitious politicians were using them to create leverage for their own interests.

This tendency of leaders to exploit the vulnerabilities and prejudices of their people to further their own ends is a great evil. It is perhaps the principal adversary that I face in my work to bring peace to South Sudan.

Over and over again, as I have traveled to the villages, kraals, and towns in my country, I have encountered people who, though they have suffered unjustly, still long for peace. They long for it so strongly that, time and again, they have demonstrated their willingness to put aside their own pain and pride in order to join hands with people on the opposite side who have the same wish for reconciliation.

And yet, time and again, these noble desires of the people are derailed, shunted aside by the maneuvering of politicians and would-be leaders. The great tragedy is that when violence erupts, as it inevitably will in such situations, it is easily labeled as "just another instance of ancient tribal hostility."

When I speak to any group—whether my own fellow citizens or Western media and thought leaders—I tell them, "If you insist on continuing to characterize the problems in South Sudan as intertribal, you are killing our people." I believe that perpetuating the assumption that violence in South Sudan is always tribally motivated makes it easier for the West to ignore the situation altogether. "Oh, well," some may say, "Jieng and Nuer have been fighting each other for hundreds of years. What can we do about it?" In this way, the involvement from the world community that we so desperately need becomes more difficult to achieve. As a result, South Sudan is left to fend for itself in the same old, harmful ways—and the cycles of violence continue.

I insist that tribal violence is not inevitable. It can be stopped, as I have personally witnessed. But it will not cease to exist as long as any-one, anywhere thinks it is incurable. And if we continue to blame our problems on tribal rivalry and fail to engage and call to account those politicians who are manipulating events from behind the scenes, we are ignoring the real root cause of the disease.[4]

Toward that end, in May 2013, just two months after the PCCPRT made its report to President Kiir, the Roman Catholic Archbishop of Sudan, Paulino Lukudu, and I went to President Kiir and Vice President Machar. For some time we had been hearing rumors of worsening ten-sions between these two leaders. The news in our committee report about persons seeking support from Machar for separatist and disruptive pol-icies was only the latest among similar, disturbing information that we had been made aware of.

Archbishop Lukudu and I went to the two leaders separately, and then together, pleading with them to do all within their power to settle their differences peacefully. Both Kiir and Machar assured us that this was their intention.

Two months later, however, the rift between the two became very public when, on July 23, President Kiir dismissed Machar as vice pres-ident, along with most of his cabinet, in what appeared to many as a purge aimed at ridding the government of dissidents within its highest ranks. In response, Machar issued many public criticisms of Salva Kiir: principally that he was developing dictatorial tendencies and that he had been heavy-handed in his dealings with those who disagreed with him.

The public rhetoric did not improve, though a meeting of the SPLM Party, to be attended by both President Kiir and Vice President Machar, was scheduled for December 14, 2013. As the time for the meeting approached and the political environment became ever more toxic, Arch-bishop Lukudu and I tried to convince Kiir and Machar to postpone the meeting until a more propitious moment. We were unsuccessful.

And then, on December 14 and 15, 2013, violence erupted in Juba, as soldiers of the SPLA loyal to President Kiir, who is Jieng, and others loyal to Riek Machar, who is Nuer, began killing each other. The violence spilled over into the town, and soon it took on ethnic dimensions, as Jieng and Nuer began fighting each other. And so, once again, a political dispute resulted in the reactivation of tribal mistrust—with deadly results. In Juba, many civilians were killed indiscriminately.

President Kiir accused Machar and his loyalists of plotting a coup, and Machar countered by accusing President Kiir of bad faith and intentions to assume sole control of the government. Once again, we were locked in a civil war, but this time, it was against fellow South Sudanese, as those who had formerly joined hands to oppose the repression of Khartoum now took up arms against each other.

In January 2014, an attack by rebel forces in Bor left thousands dead and thousands more displaced—most of them civilians, in this case, likely killed in retaliation for the earlier violence in Juba. Among those killed were many church workers—people whom I knew personally. On January 31, 2014, Most Rev. Justin Welby, Archbishop of Canterbury, visited Bor with me and prayed for the survivors of the violence. With Archbishop Welby, I walked along streets lined with dead bodies. "We stood with bodies at our feet and the smell of death around us, and we prayed," he said.[5] Archbishop Welby blessed a mass grave that would soon hold hundreds of bodies, and afterward he proclaimed that even in such desperate circumstances, he "saw God in the extraordinary fact that after half a century of civil war … we could stand in Bor and see people weeping with compassion, because the spirit of God still moves with love in their hearts."[6]

And then, in April, an attack by rebel forces in Bentiu, in Unity State near the border with Sudan, left hundreds dead. Many of the slain were in churches and mosques, where they had taken refuge. Prior to the attack, a local radio station was broadcasting messages of hate, warning non-Nuer that the soldiers were "coming for them" and urging the rape of non-Nuer women. And even so, many Nuer were also killed in Bentiu because they were judged to be trying to help those of other tribes or because they were not showing enough enthusiasm for the massacre that was taking place.[7]

As I said earlier, I could not accept this state of affairs as a failure of the peace process, because the struggle of peace must not falter. I continued to engage government, religious, and other leaders in the West as I had been doing since 2010, when I met with British Prime Minister Gordon Brown about the problems facing South Sudan. We also continued to work night and day to bring about an end to the violence. In April, President Kiir instituted the Committee for National Healing, Peace, and Reconciliation and asked me to chair the group. As chair of this committee, I worked in partnership with the South Sudan Peace and Reconciliation Commission, chaired by Chuol Rambang, and the Specialized Parliamentary Committee for Peace and Reconciliation, chaired by David Okwier.

In May 2014 I was called from a meeting of the Anglican Communion Standing Committee in London with news that negotiators with the Intergovernment Authority on Development (IGAD) were requesting my presence in Addis Ababa, Ethiopia, to take part in talks between Salva Kiir and Riek Machar. This was the first time the rivals had met face-to-face since violence erupted in Juba the previous December.

I went immediately to Addis Ababa and met with both men. When agreement on a truce was reached, I prayed publicly with them, asking God to bless this agreement so that healing and restoration might come to our suffering nation.[8]

Soon after this meeting with President Kiir and Riek Machar, I issued the following statement, on social media and elsewhere:

When the house catches fire and starts burning, everyone runs with a bucket of water in an attempt to put out the fire. Our house is burning, and it requires all of us to join hands together to quench this fire.

The armed violence which erupted in Juba on 15th December 2013, was a result of political disagreement within the SPLM party. The SPLM politicians disagreed, and the news of their disagreements reached their subjects within the national army, the SPLA, leading to military confrontations inside the military barracks in Juba. The violence quickly spread to other towns in South Sudan, leading to mass killings and displacements. Our women and children, after having been in relative peace during the [Comprehensive Peace Agreement] interim period and after independence, have once again been subjected to untold sufferings....

With a long history of armed struggle for freedom which began in 1955, when the first civil war started, and ended in 2005 through the signing of the Comprehensive Peace Agreement (CPA), we as South Sudanese have been living under miserable conditions of suffering. Regrettably, even as our people were involved in the struggle for their freedom from the North [Sudan], splits on tribal lines got in the way of the process, [and] women and children were at all times the victims.

... It is inconceivable that we are once again recalling our old, dark days.... This war, which clearly began in the kitchen of the SPLM due to political misunderstandings, was quickly labeled as a tribal conflict, pitting Nuer and Dinka as rivals. However, as a church leader, I reject this theory. Why should political grievances be translated to tribal conflicts? Why should selfish political ambitions be used to destroy the two tribes of Dinka and Nuer and South Sudan as a whole?

I have to say categorically that this is a political war of a national stature and not a Dinka and Nuer conflict, and I urge these two communities to understand this and stop killing each other for no good reason. This is a power struggle between the President on one side and Dr. Riek Machar on the other.

... As our Mothers Union leader once said, "Our house is

already burned anyway." Therefore it requires our collective efforts to rise from the ashes and see what we can salvage. On that basis, I am calling on all stakeholders, including religious leaders, civil society, women, youth, and members of the international community in South Sudan, to join us in our search for durable solution to the current crisis.

Meanwhile, peace can also come when the warring parties agree to cease hostilities and express their willingness to commit to the spirit of peaceful dialogue. I commend the government for releasing all the political detainees, and I further insist on the government to take more concrete actions aimed at bringing a lasting solution to the crisis. I am also calling on the SPLM/A in Opposition [led by Machar] to respond in good faith and do what can be done within their power to stop the ongoing violence.

There's no time for a blame game at this point, and I request former political detainees to put aside their grievances and join the rest of the country in their quest for peace and reconciliation in the country.

Our people have suffered enough, and it is high time we give peace a chance. We as the Committee for National Healing, Peace, and Reconciliation (CNHPR) urge the two warring parties to engage in active dialogue and make a speedy end to the conflict. Time is not on our side. Now is the time for peace.[9]

❖ ❖ ❖

Later that year, we launched our community-based peace process in Bor Town. We recognized, of course, that those at the high levels of government still had to do their own work toward reconciliation and compromise, but we also knew it was important to begin at the grass-roots level to build bridges between groups that had a long history of antagonism toward each other. We brought together church and community leaders and citizens from the Jieng and Nuer communities. On August 2, 2014, women's groups from Nuer and Jieng communities met together for the first time since the outbreak of fighting, the previous December.

One of our chief purposes was to have Nuer and Jieng actually talking to each other. As they did this, they discovered that those on both sides had endured similar suffering and also had similar hopes for a better future. Such dialogue is a proven way to break down the harmful stereotypes that these groups hold toward each other.

One of the women made a statement that I found very telling. Rebecca Ayen Awan, a resident of Duk County, said, "Politicians are selfish; they are destroying the future of our children.... They send their children to the best schools abroad and set our husbands and children to kill each other."[10]

A coordinator for the UN Mission in Jonglei State said of the meeting, "I'm really happy with what happened here … having representatives of the Dinka women's community and representatives of the Nuer community, coming together … to find a path towards reconciliation, forgiveness, and in order to rebuild their lives."[11]

Later than month, we met with more than 200 people from Jieng and Nuer communities in Jonglei State, including elders, youth, women, and religious leaders from both groups. In a meeting with paramount chiefs and other tribal leaders, we heard grievances from both sides, but at the same time, we heard the expressed desire and commitment to work for peace. One of the Jieng chiefs from Wanglei in Twic East County said, "We are community leaders, and a good leader does not encourage violence. I want to meet the Nuer chiefs so that I can tell them that we, the chiefs … should not mobilize our children to go to war. We, the chiefs, were the very people who could have stopped the crisis from spreading."[12]

As part of this process, I met with the leaders of the Nuer in the UN camp for internally displaced persons (IDPs) in Bor. I heard their grievances and relayed to them the messages I had received from the Jieng chiefs. We also began to put in place a plan for further engagement between the two communities that included the youth and community elders.[13]

As had been the case when we were pursuing our earlier peace and reconciliation initiative for Jonglei, we wanted to begin raising up and empowering "peace mobilizers" among the Jieng, Nuer, Shilluk, and other communities who could in turn teach others in their villages and towns the practices of peacemaking and community unification. We began this process with our first Reconciliation Workshop, held over a period of twenty-eight days in October 2014 in Yei, Central Equatoria State. We brought together eighty persons from Jieng, Nuer, Murle, Shilluk, and other tribal groups from all ten states of South Sudan and created an environment where they could talk and listen to each other, could undergo training in conflict resolution and reconciliation, and could gain the basic skills they would need to go back to their communities and teach others what they had learned. This effort to "train the trainers" was an ambitious undertaking of a kind that had never been tried before in South Sudan.

Rev. Bernard Suwa, Secretary General of the CNHPR, said of the experience, "I personally came [to Yei] loaded with anxieties and fears as to how I would keep the Dinkas and Nuers, and other tribes, together for four weeks without anything exploding. Now, to me, this unity is something that we can really celebrate. It has given me hope that left alone, away from these political challenges that we are made to drink every day, South Sudanese can find a space to live together."[14]

I told the attendees, in my opening address, "Do you know why South Sudan is fighting? It is because we identify ourselves with our tribe…. You are going to find a new identity here. And I believe that this group here, if you change, will change the whole nation of South Sudan."[15]

During the month the peace mobilizers spent in Yei, many remarkable things happened. People who did not trust each other learned not only to listen to each other, but also to understand each other's pain and hopes. Reverend Suwa noted that no family in South Sudan was free from suffering and wounds, and that all of us needed to be delivered from prejudice and mistrust in order to forgive, be reconciled, and move forward to build our nation. As the month progressed, we witnessed people weeping openly, telling their stories, singing together, playing sports together, teaching each other their particular tribal dances, and announcing and acting out their forgiveness for one another. The participants left Yei with specific plans for sharing the message of reconciliation in their communities.

The Reconciliation Workshop in Yei was the first step in our objective to train 550 ambassadors for peace who would fan out across the Republic of South Sudan, equipping others to aid the people of our nation in learning to settle their differences without resorting to violence. This effort was driven by our belief that this people-to-people approach had far greater promise of bringing about real change in our country than anything the politicians could devise.

Above all, we intended to create a peace process that was organic to the people of South Sudan. Rather than depending on a top-down approach imposed by leaders who often proved to be more motived by their own interests than by serving their people, we purposed to develop a process that would draw South Sudanese of all tribes and socioeconomic levels into a genuine discourse on their own origins, current situations, and future objectives.

We needed for our people to decide on their own what kind of country, society, and communities they wanted to have, rather than being told by someone else. Whether Egypt, one of the colonial powers, Khartoum, or our own military and political leaders, someone else had been dictating to the people of South Sudan for decades what their nation should be. We wanted to empower the people to make this all-important decision for themselves.

❖ ❖ ❖

By the end of 2014, we had been able to conduct similar initiatives in Yirol, Bor, Malakal, and Twic East County. We had established a national organization in Juba to oversee and facilitate the activities of the CNHPR.

We had conducted formal discussions with many of the former political detainees, delegations in Addis Ababa, and the government of Jonglei State.

As we moved into 2015, of course, we still faced the ongoing obstacles created by the conflict between President Kiir and former vice president Machar. The government and the SPLA were engaged in military operations against the forces loyal to Machar, which he had dubbed the "Sudanese People's Liberation Army in Opposition" (SPLA-IO). Machar's forces, in some cases assisted temporarily by local militias, held territory that included much of Upper Nile, northern and southeastern Jonglei, southern Unity, and eastern Warrap States. These circumstances naturally hindered our efforts to foster peacemaking efforts in these areas. The continuing instability also created uncertainty among many of our important donors, adding severe financial constraints to the list of barriers we had to overcome.

Despite all these problems, however, we were still able to accomplish a great deal. In January, we made a Peace Mission Trip to Lake State that was the largest mobilization of Christians there since 1938. From January 7 to 22, we traveled throughout the eight counties of the state, meeting with the youth in the cattle camps in order to appeal to them to stop killing each other and to turn instead toward forgiveness and reconciliation. In the Rumbek meeting along, more than 20,000 persons attended.

In February and March, we traveled to Kenya to meet with the South Sudanese diaspora there. We visited Nairobi, Nakuru, Eldoret, and the refugee camp at Kakuma. More than 5,500 women, youth, elders, religious leaders, and academicians attended these gatherings. I preached to them and told them that they needed to live in peace with each other. I emphasized again and again that the problems plaguing South Sudan were motivated by politics, not by tribal interests. I also met with the Episcopal Archbishop of Kenya, and we issued a joint statement calling for an end to the violence in South Sudan. Additionally, I met with the Deputy President of Kenya, William Ruto, and received his promise that Kenya would support efforts to find peaceful solutions for South Sudan. Finally, I met with elders of different tribal groups and worked with them to forge agreements to cooperate with each other in keeping peace in their communities.

At the end of March, we convened a one-week workshop in Kuajok, for the purpose of designing our upcoming peace mobilizer training in what was then Warrap State, which would begin the following month. We worked with coordinators, facilitators, lead peace mobilizers, and CNHPR staff to prepare training materials, make logistical arrangements, and confirm roles and responsibilities, in preparation for the training of the fifty-five peace mobilizers that would take place a week later, in April.

The peace mobilizers in Warrap State came from all forty-two payams and included spiritual leaders, directors of women's and youth organizations, and other community leaders. We provided them with a history of the conflict in our country and of the various peace processes that had been undertaken. We also helped them develop basic skills such as note taking, documentation of consultation, and working with the various administrative procedures that our process required. Most importantly, we trained them to facilitate community dialogue and conflict resolution and to help in identifying solutions to problems that would allow for peace to take root and grow. In May and June, those we had trained went out into the payams of Warrap State to meet with chiefs, elders, women, youth, and religious leaders, continuing the work of our people-to-people initiative.

Our plans for the rest of 2015 included peace mobilizer training sessions and payam consultations in Eastern Equatoria and Unity States, county-level conferences in Warrap State to follow up on issues surfaced during the payam consultations there, selection of peace mobilizers for Lakes, Western Equatoria, and Unity States, and a strategic review of our efforts and results on a national level, including lessons learned, progress made, and implementation of needed improvements.[16]

Meanwhile, our political leaders continue to clash, and the military and political situation in South Sudan remains unstable. In January 2014, one month after the initial violence in Juba in December 2013, representatives of President Kiir and Riek Machar met in Ethiopia and reached agreement on a ceasefire, but this pact broke down in less than a month, with renewed attacks in Bor. Then in May, Kiir and Machar met in Addis Ababa and recommitted to the truce they had discussed in January, as IGAD negotiators and I looked on. By mid-June, this agreement, too, had broken down. Similar circumstances occurred in November 2014 and January 2015; President Kiir and former Vice President Machar came to the table with announced intentions of creating a framework for reunifying the country, but each time, implementation accusations of false motives and attacks by various factions foiled implementation.

In August 2015, President Kiir signed an agreement, previously endorsed by Riek Machar, that would, among other provisions, reinstate Machar as vice president. Machar returned to Juba in April 2016, along with troops loyal to him, and was sworn in as first vice president.

Meanwhile, during that same month, a Murle militia crossed into Ethiopia and attacked a community of Nuer living there, stealing cattle and kidnapping more than 100 children. As if this were not bad enough, in July, fighting erupted outside the presidential palace in Juba while President Kiir and Vice President Machar were meeting there. More than 300 people were killed, and thousands fled the city. Though President Kiir and Vice President Machar managed to put in place a temporary ceasefire,[17] Machar soon fled Juba. Subsequently, President Kiir appointed a substitute for him, General Taban Deng Gai, who was subsequently accepted by the government as first vice president, over Machar's protests. At this time, Riek Machar remains outside the country. In August 2016, the United Nations Security Council authorized an intervention force for South Sudan, and a special court has been appointed to investigate allegations of war crimes committed during the ongoing conflict.

Meanwhile, more than a million people, many of them women and children, have fled South Sudan to escape the violence, famine, and disease.[18]

❖❖❖

Despite all this, as St. Paul wrote in Second Corinthians 4:16, "We do not lose heart." The only hope for the people of South Sudan depends upon their learning a new way to live: one that is based neither on the tribal customs of their past nor on the brutal dictates of the struggle for power. Though our land has lived through nearly constant war for the last one hundred years or more, we must teach each other what it means to live in peace. We must take up the hard work of forgiving those who have wronged us, of purposing to be reconciled, even when reconciliation is hard.

And so, the work of the Committee for National Healing, Peace, and Reconciliation goes on. As long as there are still those who are trying to divide our people from one another, we will continue our work to create unity. As long as there are those who sow hatred, we will keep on planting love in the hearts of the people. As long as forces outside our country abet and aid the violence in order to make us weaker, we will nurture forgiveness and healing, so that we may find true strength.

We have continued teaching and bringing people together to listen to one another instead of to fight. We conduct workshops, convene conferences, and work with our valuable nongovernmental supporters and partners, both domestic and international. We educate, encourage, inform, and listen, and we teach others to do the same. We will never stop.

There is still so much to do. According to a recent survey, only one-third of the people in South Sudan are familiar with the work of the CNHPR. This means that we must redouble our efforts to reach more and more people. Only when everyone has heard the message of peace, reconciliation, and healing can our nation begin waking from its long, violent nightmare.

In December 2016, President Kiir announced the institution of a national dialogue, followed by national prayers on March 10, 2017. I was privileged to lead this prayer for the nation and its people, whom I love with all my heart. With this urgent message filling my heart, I close this book with that prayer for my country and for its people. As I did on that day, I now again offer this prayer to God, knowing that with his help, South Sudan and its people can join together to become all that we are capable of being. Leaving behind the bondage of war and tribalism, we can move forward in unity toward a bright new future. God bless you all, and may God bless the Republic of South Sudan

❖ ❖ ❖

Dear Father, your word tells us that we are Christ's ambassadors. Make us true ambassadors through repentance; true ambassadors of your love; true ambassadors who forgive; true ambassadors who seek peace with one another.

Heavenly Father, we give you all the honor and praise as we celebrate the wonderful independence you have given us. You have led your children across the river, bringing an end to our slavery and abuse.

We have left behind the pain and suffering of so many years of oppression, and we know that, as you have said in your word, "Greater love has no one than this, that he lay his life for his friends." May those who surrendered their lives for the freedom we now enjoy, rest in perfect and everlasting peace in your kingdom.

Let your Holy Spirit guide and protect us as we strive for the peace, freedom, and stability we have longed for in this land. Show us how to love one another as you have so commanded us to do. Unite us to each other and to yourself.

Rid us of any plans of tribalism, corruption, injustice, division, or greed that may linger in the hearts of your children, causing us to live in darkness and confusion. And grant us your grace and blessings in abundance as we build this new nation of South Sudan for your glory, in accordance with your holy will.

We ask this in the name of Your Son, our Savior and Friend, Jesus Christ, amen.

1. Archbishop Daniel Deng Bul Yak, "Speech to Jonglei State Legislative Assembly, October 7, 2011." Papers of Archbishop Daniel Deng Bul Yak.
2. "Dachuek and Ayuel Clans of Twic East, Jonglei Reunited." *Sudan Tribune* [online], May 20, 2012. Available at http://www.sudantribune.com/ Dachuek-and-Ayuel-clans-of-Twic,42676 (accessed October 8, 2016).
3. John Chol Daau, "Minutes of Consultative Meetings of the Archbishop Daniel Deng with the Speaker of the Jonglei State Legislative Assembly, Hon. Chol Wal, September 6, 2012, in Bor Town." Papers of Archbishop Daniel Deng Bul Yak.
4. See, for example, "South Sudan's Current Conflict Leaves Residents in 'Desperate State.'" National Public Radio broadcast, August 23, 2016. Available at http://www.npr.org/2016/08/23/491103645/south-sudans-current-conflict-leaves-residents-in-desperate-state?utm_source=npr_ newsletter&utm_medium=email&utm_content=20160902&utm_ campaign=npr_email_a_friend&utm_term=storyshare (accessed August 25, 2016).
5. Carey Lodge, "Justin Welby on South Sudan: 'We Must Batter the Gates of Heaven in Prayer.'" ChristianityToday.com, May 16, 2014. Available at http://www.christiantoday.com/article/justin.welby.on.south.sudan. we.must.batter.the.gates.of.heaven.in.prayer/37502.htm (accessed October 17, 2016).
6. Matthew Davies, "Archbishop of Canterbury on the South Sudan Crisis." Episcopal News Service [online], May 14, 2014. Available at http://episco-paldigitalnetwork.com/ens/2014/05/14/video-archbishop-of-canterbury-on-the-south-sudan-crisis/ (accessed October 17, 2016).

7. Fred Barbash, "An 'Abomination': Slaughter in the Mosques and Churches of Bentiu, South Sudan." *Washington Post* [online], April 23, 2014. Available at https://www.washingtonpost.com/news/morning-mix/wp/2014/04/23/an-abomination-slaughter-in-the-mosques-and-churches-of-bentiu-south-sudan/?tid=pm_pop (accessed October 19, 2016).

8. See Matthew Davies, "As South Sudan Rivals Agree Truce, Church Plays Pivotal Role." Episcopal News Service [online], May 12, 2014. Available at http://episcopaldigitalnetwork.com/ens/2014/05/12/as-south-sudan-rivals-agree-truce-church-plays-pivotal-role/ (accessed October 17, 2016).

9. "Message from CNHPR Chairperson, His Grace Archbishop Daniel Deng Bul." South Sudan Committee for National Healing, Peace and Reconciliation Facebook Page, May 16, 2014, accessed October 18, 2016. Available at https://www.facebook.com/CNHPR/?fref=nf

10. "Jonglei's Dinka and Nuer Communities Agree to Reconcile." Gurtong [online]. Available at http://www.gurtong.net/ECM/Editorial/tabid/124/ctl/ArticleView/mid/519/articleId/15529/Jongleis-Dinka-and-Nuer-communities-agree-to-reconcile.aspx, accessed October 18, 2016.

11. "Dinka and Nuer Women Meet for Peace in Bor." Radio Tamazuj [online], August 2, 2014. Available at https://radiotamazuj.org/en/article/Dinka-and-nuer-women-meet-peace-bor, accessed October 18, 2016.

12. "Jonglei's Dinka and Nuer Communities Agree to Reconcile."

13. Ibid.

14. "Participants Hail Yei Reconciliation Workshop." *Sudan Tribune* [online], October 26, 2014. Available at http://reliefweb.int/report/south-sudan/participants-hail-yei-reconciliation-workshop (accessed October 18, 2016).

15. "A Step Together: CNHPR Begins Its Journey of Listening and Dialogue" [YouTube video]. August 4, 2015. Available at https://www.youtube.com/watch?v=PwcshzhtAIA (accessed October 12, 2016).

16. Committee on National Healing, Peace, and Reconciliation, "2015 Mid-Year Report." Papers of Archbishop Daniel Deng Bul Yak.

17. "South Sudan Clashes: Salva Kiir and Riek Machar Order Ceasefire." *BBC*

News [online], July 11, 2016. Available at http://www.bbc.com/news/world-africa-36763076 (accessed October 21, 2016).

18. "UN: More than One Millions Refugees Have Fled South Sudan." *Al-Jezeera.com* [online], September 16, 2016. Available at http://www.aljazeera.com/news/2016/09/million-refugees-fled-south-su-dan-160916145301080.html (accessed October 21, 2016).

Appendix

Important Events in the Life of Archbishop Daniel Deng Bul Yak

1950, January: Born in Pawooi, Twic East County, Jonglei State, Sudan

1955: Beginning of First Sudanese Civil War

1956: Sudan becomes independent from Egypt

1963: Anya Nya War begins

1967: Enters Anglican catechism classes in Malakal

1968: Flight to Khartoum

1971: Appointed as evangelist by the Anglican Church in Khartoum

1972: Addis Ababa Accord ends First Sudanese Civil War

1975: Attends course for diaconate at Bishop Gwynne College (then in Mundri)

1976–77: Ordained as deacon, conducts evangelism campaigns throughout Jonglei State

1978: Marries Deborah Abuk Atem, ordained as priest in Port Sudan

1979: Posted to Port Sudan as parish priest

1988: Consecrated as Suffragan Bishop of Kongor, working in Port Sudan Parish

1995: Enthroned as Bishop of Renk Diocese

1996: Study at Virginia Seminary (United States)

2005: Comprehensive Peace Agreements ends Second Sudanese Civil War

2007: Appointed caretaker bishop of Yei Diocese

2008, February: Elevated as fourth Archbishop and Primate of Sudan

2011: Passage of national referendum on independence for South Sudan, appointed chair of Committee for Peace in Jonglei State by Sudan Council of Churches

2012: Appointed chair of South Sudanese National Committee for Healing, Peace, and Reconciliation; received nomination from Chatham House (England)

2013: Outbreak of South Sudanese Civil War

Launch of community-based peace process in Yei, Central Equatoria State

Ministry Teams in Renk Diocese, 1992–2007

Pastors: Rev. John Bul Atem, Ven. Abraham Noon Jiel, Rev. Sapara Adeer Kuir, Rev. Joseph Garang Atem (later ordained as Bishop of Renk Diocese), Rev. Barnaba Madul Juac, Rev. Sapana Mawut Bol, Rev. Paul Ajang Thiel, Rev. Peter Atem Jok

Evangelists: Rev. Michael Miakol Lang, Reuben Chol Yung, Peter Chuol Mabut

1992 Renk Area Diocesan Council

Rt. Rev. Daniel Deng Bul Yak (chair), Abraham Thiong Akuei (secretary), Late Rev. Jacob Ajak Deng, Mr. Bior Kuer Aguer, Joseph Mading Ajing, Daniel Atem, Den Awan Atem, Samuel Lueth Agot, LR Grace Isaiah, Solomon Makuac Agot, Sultan Deng Anyeith, LR James Aboy Amul, LR Gordon Mathews, LR Golver Barnaba

Renk Diocese Lay Leadership

Amos Awan de Gak (1994–99), Diocesan Development; Duom Kuol Ageer (1996–2000), Financial Advisor; Lucy Small Mogga (1996–2000), Secretary and Office Manager; Majok Mading Majok (1996–2000), Diocesan Chancellor; Dora Agrey, Secretary and Office Manger for Diocesan Bishop

Committee for Renk Diocese Constitution

Hon. Abel ALierkwai, Member, International Court of Justice, The Hague, Netherlands

Justice John Wuol Makuac, Member, Supreme Court of Appeals, Sudan

Justice Maker Koat, Member, Supreme Court of Appeals, Sudan

Prof. Yithaya Ajang Bior, Senior Administrator and Lecturer, University of Juba

His Excellency Yithaya Achol De Dut, Former Sudanese Ambassador to India and South Korea

Mr. Nathiel Anai Kur, Minister of Education, Member, High Executive Council, and Former Commissioner of Jonglei, South Sudan

Mr. Alier Agot, Elder, Episcopal Church of Sudan and Postmaster General of South Sudan

Mr. Amos Awan De Gak

Mr. Duom Kuol Ageer

Text of Ceasefire Agreement with Gen. George Athor

Ceasefire Framework Agreement between the Sudanese People's Liberation Army (SPLA) and Lt. Gen. George Athor's forces

Malakal, Upper Nile State, Southern Sudan

5 January 2011

PREAMBLE

Fully committed to the consolidation of peace, stability, and security in southern Sudan; Aware that the lack of these critical ingredients puts at risk the major historical achievement of the people of southern Sudan, which is the exercise of the right of self-determination in a free and fair and internationally supervised referendum; Determined to put to an end to all acts of violence within southern Sudan, that may jeopardise the attainment of this goal; Conscious of the fact that this crisis was triggered by infighting within the same political organization, SPLM, which induced military confrontations within the SPLA, and to which the parties have expressed unconditional allegiance; Determined to peacefully resolve all armed conflicts and military confrontations through dialogue; Resolved to put into practise the executive pardon decree issued by the president of the Government of the Republic of South Sudan (RSS) with regard to incidents in Pigi and Pibor Counties of Jonglei State and other similar incidents in Unity and Upper Nile States; Cognizant of the fact that the gains of the recent All-South Political Parties Consensus-Building Conference, held in Juba, and the milestone that it laid for the smooth birth of an independent State of South Sudan should the vote in the referendum confirm secession.

Now, we, the undersigned parties to the following ceasefire framework, agree to the following:

1. GENERAL AND FUNDAMENTAL PROVISIONS

1.1 The parties have duly agreed to collaborate to observe and respect the ceasefire agreement and resort to their own wisdom to contain and solve any problem that may arise;

1.2 The parties shall refrain from any act or acts that may in any way destroy the ceasefire agreement; They shall perpetually create and uphold a favourable atmosphere for peace and tranquility;

1.3 The ceasefire agreements shall ensure clarity by eliminating any room for ambiguity in elements of the ceasefire agreement;

1.4 The ceasefire agreement shall guarantee the free movement of civilians, goods, and services in the ceasefire zones;

1.5 The parties through the joint coordinating committee (JCC) shall, within the ceasefire agreement zones, provide and share information and statistics on their arms, military equipment, and the strength of their troops, and any other relevant information;

1.6 The parties shall commit themselves to release all prisoners of conflict in their custody;

1.7 The parties shall commit themselves to render and facilitate humanitarian assistance through creation of conditions conducive to the provision of urgent humanitarian assistance to affected communities and to the displaced persons and affirm their right to return to their respective areas;

1.8 The parties agree to inform the rank and file of the armed forces as a way of popularizing ceasefire;

1.9 The parties shall commit themselves that the forces and troops under their respective commands at all levels of rank and file shall equally and fully cease fire and end hostilities;

1.10 The parties shall work to promote and disseminate peace culture and confidence building among and between the people as well as within their forces as a fundamental part of the ceasefire agreement and sustaining of peace;

1.11 The parties agree to not arm, train, recruit, or harbour on their respective areas of control or render any form of support to external subversive elements or internal armed groups.

2. ENTRY INTO FORCE

The ceasefire agreement between the parties shall come into effect from the day of signature of the ceasefire agreement (referred to as D-day).

3. THE PARTIES OF THE AGREEMENT

The parties of the agreement shall be:

3.1 The Sudan People's Liberation army (SPLA), with all its formations and units, and

3.2 Lt. Gen. George Athor, with all his formations and units.

4. PRINCIPLES OF THE CEASEFIRE

4.1 The parties agree to a permanent ceasefire among all their forces with the broader objective of sustaining the ending of the current conflict between the parties, promoting peace culture, reconciliation, and confidence building among the people of Southern Sudan;

4.2 The permanent cessation of hostilities shall include final termination of the following activities:

4.2.1 Any military activities, including troop movement, reconnaissance, reinforcement, recruitment, air dropping, and military exercise;

4.2.2 Notwithstanding the stipulations of article 4.2.1, administrative movements that are deemed necessary and verified by the joint coordinating committee shall be jointly authorised by the parties;

4.2.3 Land, air, and river operations;

4.2.4 Laying of mines and other subversive activities;

4.2.5 Use of force against and abuse of civilians;

4.2.6 Replenishment of ammunitions, weapons, and other lethal or military equipment;

4.2.7 Hostile propaganda from inside and outside countries;

4.2.8 Occupation of new locations;

4.2.9 Any other actions that may impede the normal progress of the cease fire process.

5. THE CEASEFIRE ZONES

For the purposes of this ceasefire agreement, the ceasefire zones shall encompass the following areas:

5.1 Pigi and Pibor Counties in Jonglei State;

5.2 Shilluk Kingdom;

5.3 Mayom and Koc Counties of Unity State.

6. SCOPE OF THE CEASEFIRE

6.1 The ceasefire activities shall be divided into two phases:

6.1.1 Phase 1 Transit points

The following transit points are agreed by the parties;

6.1.1.1 Obay, for Shilluk Kingdom;

6.1.1.2 Pading, for Luo Nuer Area;

6.1.1.3 Kai, for Gawar Area.

6.1.2 The period of temporary gathering of General Athor's forces into transit points shall extend for a period of not more than seven days from the day of signing of this ceasefire agreement.

6.1.3 Phase II Assembly Areas

Lieutenant General Athor's forces shall assemble, pending integration process, in the following areas:

6.1.3.1 In Jonglei (a) Pigi County: Korwai, Kol-Nyang, and Kol-liet, while the two forces collocate in Dor; and (b) in Pibor Country, General Athor's forces shall assemble in Partet.

6.1.3.2 In Unity State, the two forces shall co-locate in Wang-Kai.

7. VIOLATIONS

7.1 The following acts shall constitute violations to this ceasefire agreement:

7.1.1 Any acts that may breach this ceasefire Agreement;

7.1.2 Any unauthorised movement and deployment of troops;

7.1.3 Any unauthorised recruitment, air dropping, and/or mobilisation drive;

7.1.4 Any unauthorised replenishment of military equipment and supplies;

7.1.5 Hostile acts that may aggravate confrontation;

7.1.6 Violation of human rights, humanitarian law, and obstruction of freedom of movement and civil population;

7.1.7 Hostile propaganda and media contention;

7.1.8 Espionage, sabotage, and acts of subversion to undermine either party and/or the cease fire agreement.

8. DISENGAGEMENT

8.1 There shall be lines of disengagement according to the assembly areas;

8.2 On the declaration of the ceasefire, the forces of the SPLA and the forces of Lt. Gen. George Athor shall maintain their current positions;

8.3 All the forces shall remain in their current positions and go to agreed assembly areas between D-Day and D-Day+5;

8.4 All the forces shall be engaged separated, encamped in their assembly points, waiting for integration.

9. PERMITTED ACTIVITIES

In view of negative consequences of the strife between SPLA and Lt. Gen. George Athor's forces, the key principle underpinning permitted activities shall be to alleviate the effects of the conflict on the civilians and the affected areas and to galvanise popular support for peace. Permitted activities shall include:

9.1 Humanitarian activities such as securing unimpeded access to humanitarian relief according to agreed regulations;

9.2 Socioeconomic activities such as assisting free movement of civilians, goods, and services;

9.3 Free movement with permits of unarmed soldiers in plain clothes who are on leave, medical referrals, or visiting their families;

9.4 Administrative movement, which includes the supply of non-lethal items (food, water, medicine, medical evacuation, fuel, oils, lubricants, stationery, and uniforms, etc.).

10. JOINT COORDINATING COMMITTEE

10.1 Shall be composed of the equal membership from the SPLA and Lt. Gen. George Athor's forces;

10.2 Shall facilitate the movement of troops to assembly areas, organise logistics, and supply and any other arising needs.

11. CEASEFIRE AND MONITORING COMMITTEE

11.1 Where and whenever deemed necessary, the ceasefire joint coordinating committee (CJCC) shall seek support from the existing CPA ceasefire monitoring mechanisms.

This framework was signed by Brig. Gen. Micheal Majur Aleer for the Sudan People's Liberation Army (SPLA), Maj. Gen. Abraham Thon Chol for the forces of Gen. George Athor, and I [Archbishop Daniel Deng] witnessed as chairman, High-level Committee for Reconciliation and Mediation.[1]

Text of the Resolutions and Recommendations of the Jonglei State Communities Conference for Peace, Reconciliation, and Tolerance

Preamble

We, the eighty four (84) chiefs, elders, women and youth representing all eleven counties and all six communities of Jonglei State met in the Jonglei State Communities Conference in Bor from 1st –5th May 2012. Prior to this members of the Presidential Committee held consultations and mini-conferences in the four former districts of Akobo, Bor, Fangak and Pibor.

The Conference was also attended by His Excellency Governor Kuol Manyang Juuk; national and state ministers; members of the national and state legislative assemblies; chairpersons of national commissions; County Commissioners; religious leaders; intellectuals; UNMISS; international observers and experts; and was organised by the Presidential Committee for Peace, Reconciliation and Tolerance in Jonglei State.

Taking note of the insecurity along our border with the Republic of Sudan, the Conference expresses its concern at the aggressive behaviour of the government of Sudan, continuing bombardment of innocent civilians, and its support for rebel militias in the Republic of South Sudan.

The Conference expressed its concern and alarm at the worsening conflict and insecurity amongst the communities in Jonglei State, and affirmed its desire and commitment for peace, reconciliation, tolerance and peaceful coexistence.

The Conference appreciates the initiative of His Excellency the President of the Republic in setting up the Committee for Peace, Reconciliation and Tolerance in Jonglei State.

The Conference welcomes the decision of the national government to disarm civilians in throughout the country and particularly in Jonglei State, and pledges its support for comprehensive disarmament.

The Conference appreciates the positive role of the Sudan People's Liberation Army for the increased security and protection and for its responsible conduct during the disarmament campaign.

Problem Statement

The Conference identified the following problems which need to be addressed to bring a sustainable peace:

1. Aggression by Republic of Sudan against Republic of South Sudan
This was identified as a major problem for peace, stability and development in South Sudan.
2. Insecurity caused by conflict between communities
Serious conflict has taken place between various communities, and has escalated recently. Of particular concern are attacks by Murle on other communities
3. Killing of vulnerable persons (including children, women, elderly, disabled)
    The scale of fighting has escalated, with the killing and mutilation of women, children, elderly and disabled being killed. This is different to traditional conflicts.
4. Abduction of women and children, whether by violence, theft or trafficking
    Abduction of women and children is a major problem. In some

cases they are kidnapped rather than abducted violently, and sometimes they are trafficked.

5. Theft of livestock

Theft and looting of livestock is a major source of conflict between communities.

6. Under-development

Lack of basic services, schools, medical facilities, roads, water points for humans and livestock, telecommunications, etc has been identified by all communities as a factor in causing conflict.

7. Unemployment

Alternative livelihoods for youth are needed so that they can be encouraged to refrain from cattle raiding and fighting.

8. Trauma

Individuals and communities have been traumatised by decades of civil war as well as the inter- communal conflicts.

9. Food insecurity

Food insecurity is both a cause and a result of the conflicts.

10. Internal displacement

Internal displacement is also both a cause and result of the conflicts.

11. Border disputes

There are a number of disputes between communities over borders and also water and grazing rights which contribute to conflict.

12. Government and administration issues

While not within the mandate of this Conference to address these issues directly, various issues relating to government and administration have been identified by the communities and are noted here for the responsible authorities to consider.

13. Other issues

Some issues have been identified which do not fit into any of the above categories.

Resolutions

In order to address these problems, the Conference makes the following Resolutions:

A. Aggression by the Republic of Sudan against the Republic of South Sudan

The Conference condemns the barbaric aggression against the Republic of South Sudan by the Republic of Sudan, supports the President, government and SPLA in resisting this aggression, and affirms that the people of Jonglei State stand ready to fulfil their patriotic duty in the defence of the nation.

B. Insecurity caused by conflict between communities
   a) Sensitisation to create awareness amongst the Murle.
   b) Combat woman and child abduction and trafficking.
   c) Promotion of intra/inter-community interactions, sports, workshops, conferences, marriage, follow-up teams, etc.
   d) Meetings between cattle camp youth.
   e) Murle to distance themselves from David Yau Yau rebel forces.

C. Killing of vulnerable persons (including women, children, elderly, disabled)
   a) Stop wanton killing.
   b) Waive compensation for those killed in the past.
   c) Compensation for those killed since the beginning of disarmament, as a deterrent.

D. Abduction of women and children, whether by violence, theft or trafficking
   a) Tracing and identification of abductees.

b) Immediate return of abductees where possible.

c) Regularisation of status by negotiation for those who cannot be returned.

d) Registration of births, marriages, and deaths.

E. Theft of livestock

a) Community policing.

b) Amnesty for cattle stolen in the past.

c) Chiefs to control thieves, raiders, and abductors.

d) Bride price to be discussed in each community.

F. Trauma

a) Sports activities.

b) Social transformation of youth through moral and religious orientation.

c) Encouraging forgiveness and reconciliation at every level, including political parties, civil society, faith communities, etc.

G. Border disputes

a) Grazing and water rights need to be negotiated by joint committees of chiefs.

H. Other issues

a) Luo Nuer to continue distancing themselves from the prophet. Other communities should deal appropriately with their kujurs.

b) Enlightenment of the people so that they do not follow those (such as David Yau Yau) who rebel against the government.

Recommendations

A. The Conference also makes the following Recommendations: Insecurity caused by conflict between communities

1. Enforcement of law and order.

2. Effective buffer zones.

3. Aerial surveillance.

4. Roads andc ommunications.

5. Closure of illegal sources of firearms.

5. Implementation of Bentiu Accord (armed chiefs' guards).

6. Recruit youth leaders into organized forces.

7. Address the issue of Murle criminals already in other communities' territory.

8. Alcohol production, sale and consumption must be regulated.

9. SPLA should continue with comprehensive disarmament.

B. Killing of vulnerable persons (including women, children, elderly, disabled)

1. Arrest and trial of culprits.

2. Government to protect civilians.

3. Government should address threats by armed insurgents.

C. Abduction of women and children, whether by violence, theft or sale

1. Enforcement of rule of law to prevent abduction and trafficking.

2. Trial of culprits, including traffickers, and severe punishment.

D. Theft of livestock

1. Anti–stock theft unit.

2. Deployment of police.

3. Regulation of movement of livestock at borders between payams, counties, and states.

4. Enhancing equipment of security forces.

5. Aerial surveillance.

6. Recovery and return of stolen livestock.

7. Arrest and trial of culprits.

E.   Under-development
1. Equitable sharing of resources.
2. Schools and health centres.
3. Roads.
4. Telecommunications.
5. Strengthening local administration.
6. Health centres.
7. Water points for humans and animals.

F. Unemployment
1. Create employment opportunities.
2. Reformatory/rehabilitation school.
3. Absorb youth into organized forces.
4. Equitable employment.
5. Exploitation of natural resources.
6. Farming.
7. Income-generating activities.

G.   Trauma
1. Individual and community counselling.
2. Creation of conducive living conditions.
3. Address special needs, including disability.
4. Use of mass media.

H.   Food insecurity
1. Provide security so people can produce food.
2. Veterinary drugs.
3. Dissemination of weather early warning reports.
4. Resttlement and rehabilitation of displaced persons.
5. Road infrastructure.
6. Food support to vulnerable groups.

7. Provision of tools, improved seeds, and agricultural training.

8. Microfinance schemes.

9. Cooperatives.

10. Managing floods and other natural disasters.

I. Internal displacement

1. Relief, resettlement and rehabilitation of IDPs.

2. Provision of security.

3. Provision of orphanages.

J. Border disputes

1. Expedite border demarcation between payams, counties, and states.

2. State to regulate payam and county boundaries.

3. Security to be provided to facilitate movement and trade across international border with Ethiopia.

K. Government and administration issues

1. Empower men to traditional leadership.

2. Government to treat all communities equally.

3. Governor should visit all communities regularly.

4. Creation of new counties and states to be discussed.

5. Location of state capital to central area should be discussed.

6. Location of some county HQs to be discussed.

7. Provision of prisons in the counties.

8. Provision of judges and public prosecutors; construction of courts in the counties.

9. Upgrading of unqualified civil servants through capacity-building.

10. Payment of salaries to chiefs.

L. Other issues

1. Demining.

2. Akobo River to be dredged.

3. Land issues of the Anuak community in Akobo.

4. Monitoring Committee to follow up implementation of commitments and related issues.

Implementation

The Conference recognises that there have been many peace conferences in Jonglei State in the past and that many of their resolutions and recommendations are similar to the Resolutions and Recommendations of this Conference, but have not been implemented.

We, the participants in this Conference, commit ourselves to implement the Resolutions of the Conference, and urge the appropriate authorities, the political leadership and the citizens to take seriously the Recommendations.

The Conference has prepared a Plan of Action (attached as an appendix) which identifies who is responsible for implementing each of the Resolutions and Recommendations.

Follow Up

The Conference believes that peace is a process and that for the fruits of this conference to be fully enjoyed by the people of Jonglei State there must be monitoring and follow-up implementation. Hence the Conference humbly recommends His Excellency the President to consider how this follow-up can best be achieved.

Conclusion

We, the participants in the Conference, representing the six communities of Jonglei State:

- Commit ourselves to peace, reconciliation and tolerance amongst our communities.

- Commit ourselves to these Resolutions.
- Appeal to our national and state governments to assist and to ensure that they are implemented.

Signed by the Paramount Chiefs and other Chiefs of Jonglei State on behalf of the six communities of the State, in Bor Town, Jonglei State, 5th May 2012[2]

Minutes of Consultative Meetings of Archbishop Daniel Deng with Speaker of the Jonglei State Legislative Assembly, Hon. Chol Wal, September 6, 2012, Bor Town

Attendance

1. Archbishop Daniel Deng – Chairing
2. Hon. Chol Wal, Speaker
3. Hon. Awol Gaijang Awol
4. Hon. Matthew Matiok
5. Bishop Ruben Akurdit Ngong
6. Rev. John Chol Daau – taking notes>

The meeting opened with prayers by Bishop Ruben Akurdit of ECS Bor diocese

Archbishop introduced the agenda of the meeting.

Introductions by His Grace Daniel Deng:

As you are all aware, early this year, the President of the Republic of South Sudan H. E. Salva Kiir Mayardit formed Presidential Committee for Peace, Reconciliation and Tolerance to help communities in Jonglei resolve their conflicts. His Excellency the President asked me to chair the committee. In May 2012, in Bor, six communities of Jonglei state signed a peace treaty to end hostilities against each other and to cease from raid of cattle and abduction of children and women. This was achieved after various levels of conferences and consultative meetings for peace dialogues.

It was noted with greater concern that the delegates from Paweny never attended any of the conferences whether concurrent or joint. Although some delegates came from Luach, Thoi and Rut. It was cited that the delegates feared a violent attack from members of their communities they have been in conflict. However, the Jonglei Joint Conference resolved that the issue of Pigi will be addressed separately.

As a result, a final report of the Jonglei Peace Conference was compiled to the president. In the final reports of the Presidential Committee for Peace, Reconciliation and Tolerance, Pigi, Twich East and Pochalla counties were reported to have remained with unresolved issues which require immediate attention.

After the president has received and studied the reports, he gave another mandate for the committee to monitor the implementation of the Jonglei Communities resolutions and to address issues of Pigi County, Pochalla and Twich East Counties. In his latest mandate to the committee, he urged the committee to urgently attend and mediate over the outstanding conflicts in the mentioned counties.

Therefore, three members of including Hon. Philip Thon Leek, Rev. Tut Nyang, Margaret Gola assisted by two technical personnel Taban Charles and Gachora Ngunjiri were tasked for monitoring and evaluation of the peace progress in Jonglei. The following were also tasked to follow on the crisis in Pigi, Twich East and Pochalla:

1. Archbishop Daniel Deng, Chairperson
2. Hon. Dr. Haruun Lual Run, member
3. Hon. Anne Kimo, Member
4. Rev. John Chol Daau, Secretary

Following the composition of this committee, the chair, His Grace Daniel Deng initiated consultative meetings with intellectuals from Pigi to share ideas on how to address the issue of Pigi. The first meeting was with Hon. Gier Chuang. His response was positive and acknowledged that there is crisis in Pigi County. He acknowledged that there have been grievances and he recommended that the communities of Pigi should reconcile, since it won't help the communities to continue in conflict. Hon Gier pledged to make every effort to bring together the communities of Pigi for peace dialogue. Hon. Gier requested if I could meet them first separately with Kuol Chol Awan. I brought the two together in my office after which they agreed to bring about peace in their communities and to mobilize their communities for peace dialogue. Gier and Kuol expressed fears that there are other communities invading some territories of the people of Pigi.

In these consultative meetings, Hon. Gier Chuang Aluong, Kuol Chol Awan, Joshua Dau Diu and John Antipas Ayiei have consented that an initiative for peace dialogue and reconciliation must be pursued in Pigi. They have all acknowledged that there is crisis in Pigi and there is need for peace to prevail among these communities. All cried out that reconciliation is needed among the communities of Pigi. All have expressed bitterness and past grudges but committed that there must be a way forward to achieve reconciliation.

Therefore, we resolved to bring together intellectuals from four sections of Rut, Luach, Thoi, and Paweny. Before bringing together the intellectuals, a prior meeting with Joshua Dau Diu, John Antipas Ayiei and Speaker Chol Wal was considered a prerequisite. I have met with Joshua, John Antipas, and both have confirmed and acknowledged that there must be peace among the communities of Pigi. They strongly recommended Pigi and Ataar Intellectual Forums to take place in Juba as soon as possible.

It is our turn with you today.

Hon. Chol Wal

Many thanks archbishop for great efforts to pursue reconciliation among the Padang people. I acknowledged that Jonglei is a little calm at the moment as a result of the peace conference held in Bor some few months ago. However, Chol warned that not all are for peace in the communities even though all may speak and promise to work for peace. The appointment of the commissioner was a contentious issue but we urged that people should not be refused on the basis of their clans or tribes but on the basis of their failure in delivery of services required.

Fortunately, the people of [indistinct] received their new commission but urged that there must be peace. The issue of Pigi has been dragging for a long time between the late George Athor and Gier Chuang. At the moment, the issue has grown bigger among the intellectuals and politicians.

The division of the county has also been a point of contention, but we do urge the community leaders that this should not be a major obstacle to the community peace.

People must iron out issues of conflict and embrace peace. The politicians must talk and agree. We do support the idea that the intellectuals must dialogue in their conference separately before we meet the entire community.

I fear that some individual politicians may not be as frank as we would assume. I am concerned about the developing situation between Hon. Dau Diu and Hon Gier Chuang. They may not want to agree or reconcile. However, I do consider that peace of the community is important and must be considered first than the leadership differences and interest.

Consider that the issue of Pigi is not as simple as some people may think. It is a concern. We must work hard and provide all efforts to see to it that peace comes to Pigi. Whoever will be found not for peace must be identified and reported to the highest of authority of the nation.

Currently, there are developing scenarios of communities boundaries. The neighboring communities of Nuer are invading the lands of Padang communities. This must be looked into in addition to the already existing conflict of Padang communities.

Hon. Matthew Matiok

The problem in Pigi is greatly fueled by incitement of politicians in Juba. I strongly support the idea of intellectual conference in urban areas. The communities back home are innocent.

People must listen to one another. We commend archbishop for his concern to resolve issues of conflict among the communities. Right now people are visiting one another between Korfulus and Ataar, that is a good sign of peace and it must be enhanced to cultivate greater environment for peace.

People are experiencing hunger back home due to insecurity they have created to themselves. I recommend that the four leaders including Gier, Dau, Johnny and Antipas must be present in the intellectual consultative meeting,

Hon. Awol Gaijang

The communities are willing to meet for peace but it is the politicians who are not happy for it.

Back home, the communities are facing problems of lack of basic services. They are unable to cultivate due to insecurity they have created among themselves. I strongly believe the politicians are inciting the communities. We must identify those who are behind the problem of the Pigi. The government must know them.

Bishop Ruben Akurdit

Pigi is an important area of the nation of South Sudan. It is on the first page of South Sudan history.

We must work for peace to enable children and women of Pigi experience peace and harmony.

The unfortunate thing is that when your children will feel ashamed of the leadership of their forefathers. This must not be allowed to happen. We must work hard to change the trend of conflict and rewrite the history for peace. We must record history of peace for the benefit of future generation. We must continue praying that peace must prevail in Pigi and we shall be proud.

[Meeting ended with prayers]

Findings and Recommendations of the Consultative Meetings

- The crisis started way back between senior commanders Mayar and George Athor. Although attempts were made to reconcile them by the HQs of Late Dr. John Garang, there was no success in resolving their differences.
- It was alleged that perhaps the presence of Cdr Gier in Garang's HQs by then might have interfered with the process and mediation attempts by the HQs.
- It is also alleged that late George and Gier rivaled over leadership of who to represent their community. An example is cited when they celebrate concurrently after their appointments into with Gier appointed minister and George promoted to high military rank.
- It has been reportedly said that some SPLA officers from the section of Paweny were executed by George Athor.
- Hon. Gier has also been accused of not respecting the elders of Pigi Community.

- The intellectuals have repeatedly emphasized the issue of land invasion by the surrounding communities (Shilluk, Lak, Gawer and Low Nuer) invading the land of Pigi communities. The mentioned communities have encroached into the land of the Pigi communities.
- The intellectuals have unanimously agreed that there must be reconciliation among the communities of Pigi.
- In the consultative meetings, all the intellectuals have acknowledged and accepted that there is crisis in Pigi county and must be address.
- All have agreed to hold intellectual conference first before the community conference

Conclusions

- I have recommended that the meeting of intellectuals from Pigi County will be conducted before meeting with the communities. This will help us to sift and scrutinize issues in a smaller group before we meet the larger community. By having this conference we may have a way forward for the community reconciliation.
- There will be selected participants to attend the intellectuals consultative meetings in Juba, and Malakal
- Issues must be separated from people
- Issues connected to late George Athor and his rivals in the community are considered to have triggered the conflict. Some of them concerned George Athor and Gier Chuang must be addressed carefully.
- There are past issues of people lost lives in various crises as a result of differences between Gier and Athor.
- Intellectual Consultative Meeting of Pigi intellectuals must take place soon.

- List of intellectuals to be developed as soon as possible. The list will compose of intellectuals from Bor and Juba representing Luach, Thoi, Rut and Paweny. Ten intellectuals from Bor will attend joining the rest of intellectuals in Juba. A forum will not exceed thirty intellectuals.
- After the meeting in Juba, there will be another consultative meeting with intellectuals and community leaders in Malakal to disseminate and share the ideas and resolutions of Juba meeting.
- There will be five days Greater Fangak community conference for peace dialogue to take place between December 2012 and January 2013.
- After these meetings, resolutions and recommendations must be compile and presented to the president of the republic of South Sudan.
- After peace and reconciliation conferences, there will be a continuous follow up on implementations.

Lists of intellectuals from Bor:

Luach Community
Rt. Hon. Peter Chol Wal
Hon. Matthew Matiok Lem
Mr. James Aguer Awer
Paweny Community
Hon. Awuol Gaijang Awuol
Hon. Rebecca Arop Chuang
Mr. Lual Monyluak Dau
Mr. Ebona Majok Baguot
Rut Community
Mr. Santino Malual Meat
Mr. James Mijok Mun

Thoi Community
Mr. Anthony Malang Yak</LIST>

Lists of intellectuals from Juba

Rut Community
Peter Kuol Chol Awan
John Agany Tang
Joseph Mijak Monykuer
Akim Monykuer Awuok
Isaiah Chol Chuang
Thoi Community
John Antipas Ayiei
Peter Philip Chuang
Nyok Mijok Garkuoth
Gabriel Monynak Monywach
Anthony Malang Yak

Committee to act as recorders

- Invitation will be in writing (letters of invitations to be send out)
- Venue in Juba: Commission for South Sudan Reconstruction and Development
- Participant numbers: Thirty five participants in each forum separately.
- Budget: Fuel, lunch, teas
- Date: one of the Saturday and Sunday after
- Time : Saturday morning from 10am to 2pm, and afternoon Sunday from 2pm
- The discussion approach:

- Problem identification and statement
- Resolutions and recommendation[3]

Text of Presidential Order to Form the National Committee for Healing, Peace, and Reconciliation

1. Title and Commencement

The order shall be cited as "The Republic order No.05/2013 for the **Formation of the National Reconciliation Committee for Healing, Peace, and Reconciliation Conference** 2013" and shall come into force on the date of its signature by the President of the Republic.

2. Order

In exercise of the power conferred upon me under article 101 (j) of the Transition constitution of the Republic of South Sudan, 2011 AD, I, General Salva Kiir Mayardit, President of the Republic of South Sudan, do hereby issue this Republic order for the **Formation of the National Reconciliation for Healing, Peace and Reconciliation Conference,** composed of Members as hereunder:

1. His Grace Arch-bishop Dr .Daniel Deng Bul Chairperson
2. His Lordship Bishop Paride Taban Deputy Chairperson
3. His Lordship Bishop Rudolf Deng Majak Member
4. His Lordship Bishop Enock Tombe Member
5. Moderator Peter Lual Gai Member
6. Representative from Muslim Community Member
7. One from each of the Ten states of South Sudan Member
8. One Representative of the Women Organisation Member
9. One Representative from the Youth Organisation Member

10. One Representative from the Civil Society organisation Member

3. The Terms of Reference for the National Conciliation Committee

1. The terms of reference for the committee shall be as here under:-
   (a) To develop objectives of National Peace and Reconciliation.
   (b) To determine short term and Medium Term activities.
   (c) To Research Modern and Traditional Conflict resolution.
   (d) To liase with the Government to provide security, financial support and Mobility.
   (e) To solicit funding from local and International bodies and to seek their expertise.
   (f) To form consultative body comprising of South Sudanese elders as advisory body

2. The committee may, where it deems necessary co-opt any relevant member or members, and may form sub-committees at the state level

3. The committee shall be an independent body which shall not be subject to control and direction from anybody or any instution;the role of the Government shall be facilitative and provide support where necessary and when called upon.

4. All bodies previously formed and established by the Government of the Republic and tasked with National Reconciliation should immediately hand over all the documents, assets, finances at their disposal to the new committee.

Issued under my hand and seal of the Republic of South Sudan in Juba, this twenty-second day of the month of April in the Year 2013 A.D.

General Salva Kiir Mayardit
President, Republic of South Sudan, Juba[4]

1. "Text of Ceasefire Agreement with Gen. George Athor." Papers of Archbishop Daniel Deng Bul Yak
2. Document archive, Harvard University, Kennedy School of Government. Available at https://www.hks.harvard.edu/index.php/content/download/70264/1253866/version/1/file/Deng_JongleiPeaceConferenceResolutions1205.pdf (accessed October 25, 2016).
3. "Minutes of the Meeting of Archbishop Daniel Deng with the Speaker of the Jonglei State Legislative Assembly." Papers of Archbishop Daniel Deng Bul Yak.
4. "Text of Presidential Order 05/2013." Papers of Archbishop Daniel Deng Bul Yak.

www.ingramcontent.com/pod-product-compliance
Lightning Source LLC
Chambersburg PA
CBHW030417100426
42812CB00028B/2991/J